Central Asia under The Mongols:

This study deals with Central Asia under the Mongols. It begins with a critical survey of ecological factors and their impact in making Central Asia as a specific region. The author examines in details the rise of the Mongol power under Chingiz Khan and his successors. The work in particular unfolds the story of the growth of the Chaghatais' power in the region. Its focus is on the nature of Chaghatai–Qaidu regime in Central Asia and also their relations with neighbouring powers including China and India. The author for the first time brings out large commercial networks and expansion of trading activities in Cental Asia during this period. In other words this book is a significant addition to the history of Central Asia in medieval times.

G.D. Gulati, Ph. D from University of Delhi specializes in Medieval India History. At present he is Associate Professor at Satyawati College, University of Delhi. His earlier work is on *India's North West Frontier in Pre-Mughal Times* (Delhi, 1985). Besides he has contributed a number of research papers and book reviews in national and international journals. Currently is working on the biography of Chingiz Khan.

Central Asia under the Mongols

G.D. Gulati

DEV BOOKS

Published by:
Dev Books
2nd Floor, Prakash Deep,
4735/22, Ansari Road,
Darya Ganj,
New Delhi-110002
Phone : 9810236140
e-mail: devbooks@hotmail.com
website: www.devbooks.co.in

ISBN 978–81–89835–12–5
First published 2010

Printed in India

Dedicated to
W. Barthold
and
S. Nurul Hasan

Contents

Preface

THE IDEA OF THE subject came to my mind long ago when I was working for my Ph.D. thesis at University of Delhi on India's North-West Frontier during thirteenth and fourteenth centuries. While researching on this subject I had to discuss the Mongol invasions from the North West frontier and to study the Central Asian politics of that period. In this context it is necessary to mention that it was Prof. S. Nurul Hasan who advised me to take up a separate project on the Mongols in Central Asia. I began working on this and with the further support from Prof. I.H. Siddiqui from Aligarh Muslim University, the project took a definite shape.

Scholars have already done some significant work on the rise of the Mongols and their expansion in different countries of Asia and Europe. Mostly, they have dealt either with the Mongols in general or have written biographies of the Mongol emperors. Some of these studies deal with region or focus on countries such as China, Russia, Iran, Central or Inner Asia etc. Among these scholars, one can name Thomas T. Allsen, Reuven Amitai Presiss, W. Barthold, Michal Biran, J.A. Boyle, Peter Brent, J. Curtin, Richard C. Foltz, Ralph Fox, Herbert Frank, Danis Twitchett, Mansura Haidar, Gavin Hambly, Leo de Hartog, Erik Hildinger, H.H. Howorth, Peter Jackson, Linda Komaroff, Harold Lamb, George Lane, R.P. Lister, H. Desmond Martin, Beatrice F. Manz, David O. Morgan, E.D. Phillip, Michael Prawdin, Paul Ratchuevsky, Morris Rossabi, J.J. Saunders, Bertold Spular, G.Le Strange,

James D. Tracy, George Vernadsky, B.Ya Vladimirstov, Jack Weatherford, and Henry Yule. These scholars have touched different aspects of the life of the Mongols. Some have dealt with the socio-cultural and commercial aspects of the Mongols while others have reffered the destructive aspects of their invasions. Yet, I feel that there were number of question regarding them, which could be further explored. Central Asia under the Mongols saw the rise of the rivalries with China and other kingdoms. Being the meeting land between Asia and Europe, the region played an important role in the contemporary commercial networks. It also played a significant role in the political conditions and the policies of the rulers in the neighbouring countries.

An attempt is made to define the region 'Central Asia' in the introductory chapter. It is evident that the meaning went on changing from time to time due to its interaction with the regions around it or domination of the ruling classes. There has been no unanimity among the scholars about the space called 'Central Asia' however, I have included Mawarnnahr, Kashgharia, Semirechie and much of Jungaria for the purpose of the present study. The ecological features of 'Central Asia' had been important and decisive to influence the life of its people throughout history. Therefore, a brief survey has been made to highlight these features such as: mountain-system, river-system, steppe and deserts.

The next chapter takes into account the historical background of the Mongols and how Chingiz Khan unified the different tribes of Mongolia and later extended his control over China, West Asia and Central Asia. His sons and successors too conquered distant lands and created a vast empire from Korea to Hungary. It has also been discussed in this chapter, the division of the vast empire into different Khanates (kingdoms) among the sons of the great Khan.

The third chapter contains a discussion on 'Chaghatai Khanate' founded by Chaghatai, the second son of Chingiz. It included most of the Central Asian lands i.e Transoxiana,

Kashgharia, Badakshan, Balkh and Ghazni without any precise borders. The Chaghatais were the true nomadic vision of the Mongol empire and always at war with their co-brothers in Persia and China. The Khanate survived more than a hundred years under the Chaghatai-Kaidu alliance and their successors till the emergence of the Barlas Turks as power under Timur.

The relations between the Chaghatai Khanate and China under the title 'Relations with China' are examined in the fourth chapter. As noted in earlier chapter, Qaidu with Chaghatai had openly defied the imperial authority in China. They went at a continuous war for four-five years (1260-1264). Marco Polo assigns the cause of war the share of these conquests which the great Khan Qubilai had denied to Qaidu unless he paid homage at the court. He had captured Karakorum with the support of the Mongol chieftains who resented Qubilai's policy of sinification. Qubilai was ultimately compelled to accept Qaidu as the *defacto* ruler of those regions.

This is followed by a detailed discussion of the Indian Campaigns from Central Asia from time to time in the fifth chapter. The political conditions of Central Asia had always influenced the neighbouring regions. After making control over Afghanistan the Mongols of Central Asia threatened the borders of the Sultans of Delhi where the Turks had established themselves in the beginning of the thirteenth century. Mongols had entered the frontier of India in Chinghiz Khan's own life time and their pressure remained over there throughout the thirteenth and first quarter of the fourteenth century. The Sultans were compelled to take certain measures to meet this challenge. A detailed survey of the campaigns and why they could not succeed in their mission in India have been dealt in the end of chapter.

The penultimate chapter provides the account of commercial networks and activities that were going on in Central Asia. The formation of caravans, construction of caravansarais or *khans,* check-posts, various trade routes, trading- centers all are parts of this chapter. It has been shown that how the Mongols in Central Asia created conditions for the smooth flow to the trading activities throughout its cities and markets and how under their rule the silk-road revived. It was the globalization of its own time which brought the East and West together.

The 'conclusion' shows how the geo-polity of 'Central Asia' has played a pivotal role in its history. Despite constant wars with their co-brothers, the Chaghatais contributed in the world-commerce in the middle ages. It were they who could send expeditions into the distant places in India and had great impact on her polity, economy and society. The disintegration of the Mongols in Central Asia gave way to its ruling agents to emerge as new empires in the coming days. The best examples are the Uzbeks, Mughals and the Ottomans.

In the end I wish to mention that by and large I have consulted sources in India from Persian and English records. However, for literature available in other languages I have generally depended upon the translated works which exist on Central Asia. As far as the spellings of names and places are concerned I have followed A.J. Boyle's translation of *Tarikh-i-Jahan-i-Gusha.* However the original spellings are retained in case of quoted passages from other sources.

At the outset I must say that my greatest debt remains to late Prof. S. Nurul Hasan who had inspired me to undertake this work. Thanks are also due to the Indian Council of Historical Research, New Delhi for providing me sufficient funds to visit several libraries and research institutions located in Delhi, Kolkata, Aligarh and Shimla and to avail their facilities. I am deeply obliged to late Professor S.P. Gupta of Aligarh Muslim University who offered me twice visiting fellowship at the Centre of Advanced Studies, Department of History, Aligarh Muslim University. This enabled me to collect material available there for my present book. Most considerable debts are to Professor I.H. Siddiqui, from whom I have learnt a lot about the Mongols in Central Asia. I also thank Professor B.L. Bhadani, Professor R.K. Trivedi and Professor Mansura Haider of the same Centre. I am highly obliged to my friends Surjit Singh and to Shri P.N. Sahai former Librarian I.C.H.R. for his help in preparing the index. Indeed I am deeply thankful to my friend Bhagwan Josh of Jawahar Lal Nehru University for going through the whole text and making valuable suggestions.

I am thankful to Professor K. L. Tuteja of Kurushestra University, Professor Azizuddin, Dr. R.P. Bahuguna of Jamia Millia Islamia, Professor G.S.L. Devra of Kota Open University and Professor Jigar Muhammad of Jammu University for their continuous encouragement and also to thank my friend Mr. Vinod Kapoor for giving me the computer assistance. In the end I thank Mr. Pankaj D. Jain of Dev Books for the publication of this book.

G.D. GULATI

11th *June* 2010
New Delhi

1

Introduction

FRONTIERS OF ANY region are unstable and vary from age to age, shifting according to the balance of power between its own population and that of the surroundings. In the course of history the definition of a region also changes due to its interaction with the regions around it or the domination of the ruling class. 'Central Asia' had been ruled by different ethnic dynasties since ancient times hence the definitions went on changing from time to time.

Though, it is assumed to be clearly defined, there has been no unanimity among the scholars about the space called 'Central Asia'. We have to trace out the extent of the territory which the different states and 'nations' of Asia have held at different times and the different meanings in which the same name has been used. Different historians and social scientists have given different terms and definitions of 'Central Asia' on the basis of their scope for studying various aspects of its history.

The latest edition of *The New Encyclopedia Britannica* in its 15th volume enters 'Central Asia' as a separate subject. It deals with the region, history and countries of Central Asia. In the introduction it reads that the Central Asian region is located in the centre of the Eurasian land mars and extends from the Caspian Sea in the west to the border of Western China in the east. To north lies Russia, and to the south are Iran, Afghanistan and China. Central Asia consists of the republics of Kazakhstan, Turkmenistan, Uzbekistan, Kyrgyzstan and Tajikistan. These states all former republics of the Soviet Union, became independent in 1991. The basic idea behind the definition is to give an account of the five republics as mentioned. Hence, the 'Central Asia' at present is the region comprising of five republics of the Soviet Russia.[1]

It seems to be very narrow definition as far the historical geography is concerned. In terms of historical geography a more precisely delineated 'Central Asian heartland' consisted of three adjacent regions, collectively referred to by nineteenth century explorers and geographers as Russian and Chinese Turkestan. The first of these regions, known to the ancient Greeks as Transoxiana and to the Arabs as Ma wara an-Nahr (That Which Lies Beyond the River), consists of the area between the Amu Darya (the Oxus River of the Greeks and the Jayhún of the Arabs) and Syr Darya (The Jaxarates River of the Greeks and the Sayhun of the Arabs). It is an arid, semi-desert country where, before the development of large-scale irrigation projects in the 20th century, the sedentary population maintained itself by intensive cultivation of the fertile tracts bordering the Amu Darya and the Syr Darya or by cultivation of the oases, in which were situated the major urban centers such as Bukhara and Samarkand.

The second, predominantly steppe, region extends northward from the upper reaches of the Syr Darya to the valley of the Ili River and to the foothills of the ranges lying between the Altai mountains and the Tien-Shan. Bounded on the south by the line of the Tien-Shan and to the north by Lake Balkhash, this area was known to the Turks as the *Yeti Su*, the "Land of the Seven Rivers", hence its Russian name of Semirechye.

The third region, centering on the Takla Makan Desert, is bounded on the north by the Tien Shan, on the west by the Pamirs, on the south by the Kunlun Mountains, and the north east by the Dzungarian (Jungarian) Basin. Often referred to as Kashgaria, from its principal urban centre, Kashgar (K'a-Shih), the region is characterized by small oasis settlements lying between the desert and the surrounding ranges, such as Khotan (Ho-t'ien), Yarkand, Kashgar itself, and Aksu (A-k'o-su), which served as way stations on the famous Silk Road between China and the West. The map pertaining to the middle ages shown in the volume 15 concerns the present study is much relevant to us as it shows the regions of Khwarizm, Pamirs, Tienshan-Tarim Basin, Altai mountains bordering the great wall of China though it needs more explanation.[2]

In a modern study 'Central Asia' has been defined as the centre of the continent of Asia between Mongolia or China proper in the east; India, Bhutan, Nepal, Afghanistan in the south; Iran and Caspian Sea in the west and the Ural range of mountains or Russia in the north. It consists of almost two equal parts—East Central Asia (Tibet and Xinjiang) and West Central Asia (Kazakhstan, Kirgizstan, Tajikistan, Uzbekistan and Turkmenistan). According to the author there are several concepts of 'Central Asia', especially the Chinese, Indian and Iranian concepts. The Chinese concept comprehends it as Hsi Yu, the land west of China proper. China was the first country to appear in East Central Asia in the time of the first Han dynasty. According to the Indian concept, Central Asia is the land north of Himalayan and Hindukush mountains. Ladakh, although it is political part of India, is geographically part of East Central Asia. According to the Iranian concept, it is the land north of Khurasan. With the advance of Russia eastwards in the seventeenth century, there also has been the Russian and Western concepts of Central Asia as the land east of the Caspian Sea, Balkh though politically part of Afghanistan, geographically is a part of West Central Asia.[3]

Some scholars equate 'Central Asia' with 'Inner Asia' which

is the expanse of steppes, deserts and mountains that extend across Eurasia from the Caspian Sea and the Ural Mountains to Manchuria. Whereas the term 'Inner Asia' has been applied to the region which includes seven countries—the five former states of Soviet, Sinkiang and Mongolia. Basically, the five ex-Soviet Asian Republics—Kazakhstan, Uzbekistan, Turkmenistan, Tajikistan, Kirghiztan etc. represent a region formally known as Soviet Central Asia and now according to the scholars simply 'Central Asia'. Though this term has often been used to describe generally the Asian interior has now been agreed upon.

In medieval period if we divide the Chingized Empire, the Chaghatai Khanate comprised Mawarnnahr, Kashgharia, Semirechie and much of Jungaria, which is the main focus of our study. In another work the term 'Central Asia' has been used in a more broader terms. The editors have used the term of 'Central Asia' to describe the area comprising Kazakh, Kirghyz, Tajik, Turkmen and Uzbek (Ex Soviet Republics of USSR), the Mongolian's People's Republic and the three dependencies of China known today as the Inner Mongolian Autonomous Region, Sinkiang-Uighur Autonomous Region and the Tibet Autonomous Region.[4]

An identical term for 'Central Asia' has been used in yet another work and it gives a broad definition. "The geographical scope of 'Central Asia' is confined to the former Soviet Central Asian Republics of Tadjikistan, Kyrghizia, Kazakhstan, Uzbekistan and Turkemenia; Xinjiang and Tibet, Autonomous region of People's Republic of China, Mongolia and Afghanistan."[5]

'Central Asia' or 'Shredne Asia' in Russian language, is widely known as 'Middle Asia' to the Russians.[6] At another place it reads: "From the steppes of Kazakhstan to the Arabian sea and from the Caspian to the north of the Indus, this vast stretch of Asian heartland is one cultural zone where people have common religion and ethnic history. For many centuries it is this 'Central Asian land', which served as the great Silk

Road, over which passed traders and businessmen, scholars and missionaries and artists and artisans. The entire area from the Aral to the Arabian sea has actually been one great economic zone which was characterized by free trade and free movement of people. All over this region from Lahore to Kazan on the Volga and from Baku to Multan one can witness the presence of caravanserais that lined the old trade routes and facilitated large scale business."[7]

'Central Asia' as understood in restricted sense rightly should be 'Asia-i-Miana' i.e. 'Middle Asia'. It is the land that lies between China and South Asia on the east and the Ural mountain and the Caspian Sea on the west and between the Siberian forest on the north and Iran-Afghan plateau on the south i.e. the southern Oxus river line and the Kopet Dagh range on the south."[8]

Historically, this vast area which separates from the Urals to the Pamirs from the shores of the Caspian Sea to the Altai mountain was a single entity, even though its name differed (Turan, Mawarannahr, Desht-i-Kipchak, Turkestan]. During the pre-Soviet period the Central Asian Cultural Space comprised not only the aforementioned territory but also northern Iran, Afghanistan and some regions of Western China.[9]

In a recent historical study on Central Asia, the author uses the term Central Asia in his work referring the area encompassing Transoxiana and Turkistan, from the Oxus to the Altai mountains and the eastern figures of modern Xinjiang.[10] Another scholar refers to three different geographical definitions while distinct from one another, partly overlap. The first term, 'Central Asia' refers to the territories that are today occupied by the Muslim republics of former Soviet Union, along with nearby areas of Asiatic Russia, and parts of north-west China. In short, this is the area north and north-east of the province of Khurasan. The second term, 'Inner Asia' (sometimes referred to as Inner Eurasia) is employed in a wider sense, designating the vast area covered by the countries of 'Central Asia', as well as Mongolia, north-western and north-eastern China, Afghanistan and Tibet. The area referred to by third term—the Eurasian Steppes—is bordered by western Hungary in the west, Manchuria in the east, and the Siberian forest belt in the north.[11]

Yet another writer divides the region into four regions: the steppe in the north, both left and right of the middle Syr Darya; the semi-desert on the lower Syr Darya; the desert, which on the left bank of the Amu Darya is called Kara Kum (the Block Sand), and on the right bank Kyzyl Kum (the Red Sand), with occasional patches in the Farghana valley and east of the Zarafshan; and the mountains, of which the main chains are the Tien-Shan, the Alai and Trensalai, and the Pamirs, with the minor ranges along the upper Zarafshan and south of Samarqand.[12]

ECOLOGICAL FEATURES

Mountain system

Many features which include mountain-system, rivers, deserts and steppes, had always influenced the life of the inhabitants throughout its history. Among the mountains the southern border of Central Asia is marked by an almost unbroken chains of mountain ranges, nearly four thousand miles long which run from China to the Black Sea and which restricted assess in the direction of South East Asia, the Indian subcontinent and the Middle East. From East to West these ranges are the Nan Shan, the Altyn Tagh, the Kun Lun, the Karakorum, the Hindu Kush, the Paropamisus, the Elburz and the Caucasus. In other words if we see the whole plateau, in sharp somewhat of an irregular rhomboid, it is completely enclosed by six grand ranges of mountains, namely the Himalayas looking south towards India, the Pamir looking west towards Central Asia, the Altai looking north towards Siberia, the Yablonoi looking north-east towards Eastern Siberia, the

Yun-ling and the Inshan looking towards China.[13]

Its highest mountain peaks are in the Pamir region. The term Pamir which has the roof of the world, means 'pasture' in the Tajik language. Its great lakes are the Issyk Kul in Kyrghystan and Balkhash in Kazakhstan. The vast Issyk Kul, the warm water lake situated in a fold of the Tianshan range, is an inland sea. It is believed that Kyrghyzes built their first settlement there in the fourteenth century.[14] Marco Polo gives an eye witness account of the Pamir and its surroundings. He writes "traveller goes three days' journey towards the north-east, through mountains all the time, climbing so high that this is said to be the highest place, he finds a plain between two mountains, with a lake from which flows a very fine river (he does not give the name of the river). Here is the best pasturage in the world; for a lean beast grows fat here in ten days. . . . There are great quantities of wild sheep of huge size from the horns of these sheep people make bowls from which they feed . . . there are also innumerable wolves. . . . This plain whose name is Pamir, extends fully twelve days journey. In all these twelve days there is no inhabitation or shelter, but travellers must take their provision with them. No birds fly here because of the height and the cold. And I assure you that because of this great cold fire is not so bright here nor of the same colour as elsewhere and food does not cook well. At the end of this twelve days' journey, the traveller must ride fully forty days more east west east, always over mountains and along hillsides and gorges, traversing many rivers and many deserts. And in all, this journey he finds no habitation or shelter, but must carry his stock of provision. This country is called Belor (Kafiristan). The inhabitants live very high up in the mountains. They are idolaters and utter savages living entirely by the chase and dressed in the skins of beasts. They are out and out bad."[15]

Separating the Tarimbasin from the basins of Amu Darya and Syr-Darya, the Pamirs are approached from the north and west by a series of lesser ranges which enclose the valleys through which the Amu Darya and Syr Darya descend to the plains of Badakhshan, famous among medieval travellers for its turquoise and ruby mines, and fertile Farghana, home of the 'celestial horses' highly prized in T'ang China. North-east of the Pamirs and stretching far to the east towards the Gobi are the Tien Shan which separate the fertile valley of Ili and Jungaria to the north from the arid Tarim basin (Kashgharia) to the south. The Tien Shan, the Pamirs and Kun Lun enclose the later region on every side except towards the east. Unlike the forbidding Kun Lun, the Tien Shan have never prevented intercourse between the area to the north and south of them and in this respect they resemble the loftier Pamirs. Known to the Chinese as the Heavenly mountains, the Tien Shan is one of the greatest ranges of Asia, with Khan Tengri reaching a height of 23,600 feet.

To the north-east of the Tien Shan and rising to a height of some 10000 feet are the Altai, traditional home of the Turkish people and linked with the Tien Shan by a series of low ranges—the Jungarian Ala Tan and the Khrebet Tarbagatai—pierced by long valleys through which nomadic peoples have so often made their way from Jungaria or the Gobi region into what is now Kazakhstan. Further to the north and east of the Altai lie the eastern and western Sayan ranges, the mountains of Outer Mongolia and these extend almost as far as Lake Baikal. Thus, it may be said that Central Asia is divided into two halves by an uneven chain of mountain ranges running from south-west to north-east starting near Herat in western Afghanistan and ending in the neighbourhood of Irkutsk in Siberia. Friar William of Rubruck witnessed the narrow passages in the Altai mountain with bad grazing. It was extremely cold so that he and his party turned their sheepskins with the wool outside.[16]

Hindukush too, being higher mountains greatly influenced the movement of the people. Its snow once became a barrier in the movement of Chinghiz's armies when he was in the Hindukush. We find his son Chaghatai informing his father to wait for a favourable time since the road by which he was obliged to pass was covered with deep snow to an extent of about a hundred *li.*[17] Ibn Battuta tells us an anecdote which gives these mountains its name Hindukush. He writes, "There is a mountain called Hindukush, which means 'the slayer of the Indians', because the slave-boys and girls who are brought from the land of India die there in large numbers as a result of the extreme cold and the great quantity of snow."[18]

The climate of Central Asia is continental, with cold, frosty winters and excessive heat in summer. Heavy snowfalls can be expected in the north and east. Occasionally, snow also falls in the west and south but it never lies for very long. In the Kara Kum region, for instance, there may be snow and frost during the night, but the day, which follows will be sunny and hot. The winter itself is short and it is sandwiched between two rather unpleasant rainy periods, which transform the entire region into a sea of mud. Agriculture has always depended on artificial irrigation. Water is provided by rivers fed from the glaciers of Tien-Shan, the Pamirs, and the Hindu Kush. The principal crop in the oases is cotton, which was being cultivated here in the Middle Ages. Other classical crops used to be barley, millet and wheat, as well as fine vegetables. The huge melons were justly famous, they were exported, in special brass cauldrons filled with ice, to the Court of the Caliphs in Baghdad.[19]

The configuration of the mountain ranges has exercised a profound effect upon the movements of the peoples of Central Asia. At least equally decisive has been the influence of the deserts—the Ust Urt between the Caspian Sea and the Aral Sea, the Kara Kum between the Kopet Dagh (The northern escarpement of the eastern Elburz) and the Amu Darya, the Kizilkun dividing the lower reaches of Amu Darya from those of the Syr Darya, the semi-desert of the Betpak

Dala (known as the Hungry steppe) between the Syr Darya and Lake Balkhash, the immense Gobi dividing Inner and Outer Mongolia, and Takla Makan south of the Tien Shan which has been considered probably the most formidable of all the dune-covered wastes of this globe. East of the wind-eroded oasis of the Takla Makan lies the Lop-Nor and beyond that lies the Pei Shan.[20]

River system

The Amu Darya and Syr Darya which rise in the Pamir and Tien Shan ranges in the east flow into the inland Aral Sea in the north, are the great rivers of Central Asia. The ancient Greeks called the Amu Darya and Syr Darya, Oxus and Jaxartes. The Arabs called them Jihun and Sihun. About the origin of the river Amu, according to the Arab geographers was a lake in little Tibet.[21]

Al-Muqaddassi, an Arab geographer of the tenth century gives an account of the river Jayhun and the settlement on it and describes in details the course of the river, its several branches and six streams flowing into it and its various districts which people called these places as "Ma wara al-Nahr" (the area beyond the river). As for Khwarizm, this region was on both banks of the Jayhun River. The people on both sides of the river different in customs, language, disposition and natural characteristics. This was an important area, expansive, with many cities extensively built up, somewhat after the manner of the cities of Romaeans, of Sijistan, or of Kazarun. The rows of the houses were continuous as were the gardens.[22] In *Hudud al-Alam* also it has been mentioned as Jayhun which originated from Vakhan and flowing various territories in Central Asia finally fell into the sea of Khwarizm (Aral Sea).[23]

Amu Darya has several names in its upper reaches. Al-Masudi seems to be the first among the Arab geographers who contradicts the earlier belief of Ibn Khuradadhbih that river Oxus flowed into the Indus and then in to the

Abyssinian sea. He believed that Oxus flowed into the Aral sea. The Aral sea also is probably mentioned for the first time by Al Masudi.[24] The Chinese sources of the medieval period too speak of the river Amu which during these days flowed to the west of Bukhara and entered a sea called Caspian.[25] There is also a reference of floating bridge and the boats[26] and the river could be crossed in boats or floating bridge both.[27] Oxus river used to be frozen over in winter and elephants, caravans, and armies could pass over it.[28] Juvaini too refers the roads blocked due to heavy snow on the western coast of the Caspean during the Mongol campaigns into Europe.[29]

Timur's armies pursued by their enemies crossed the river Oxus on the horse back. Ahmed Ibn Arabshah highly speaks on Timur's tumultous and marvellous crossing of the Oxus and devotes a full chapter on it. He writes that Timur and his company reached the Oxus, which then-like them—was swelling beyond its bounds, and they could not delay, because their pursuers, like themselves, were ruthless. Timur therefore bade his men with all speed hurl themselves into the water, each holding the bridle and mane of his horse; and they arranged a place among themselves. He added "cross without delay and everyone who does not come to the appointed place will know that it is finished with him." Then they threw themselves and their horses into roaring waters and swelling waves, like moths flying towards a lamp. Nor did one care for another's plight or the man in front watch the fate of the man behind, and they endured the tortures of death and saw openly the terrors of destruction They emerged however, and without even a man lost collected at the place agreed.[30]

Mukaddimah inform us: "The Oxus originates at Balkh, in the eighth section of the third zone, in a great number of springs there. Large river flows into it, as it flows a course from south to north. It flows through Khurasan, then passed Khurasan to Khwarizm in the eighth section of the fifth zone. It flows into Lake Aral (the Lake of Gurganj) which is situated at foot (north?) of the city of (Gurganj). In length as in width, it extends the distance of one month's journey. The river of Farghana and Tashkent (ash-Shash), which comes from the territory of the Turks, flows into it. West of the Oxus lie Khurasan and Khwarizm. East of it lie the cities of Bukhara, al Tirmidh and Samarkand. Beyond that is the countries of the Turks, Farghana, the Kharlukh and other non-Arab nations."[31] At another place it says "The Oxus comes from the country of Wakhan in the area of Badakhshan which border on India, in the south east corner. It soon turns west to the middle of the section. There it is called the Kharnab River. It then turns north, passes Khurasan, flows due north, and finally flows into Lake Arab.[32]

Hamadullah Mustawfi gives a more clear and detailed account of the river.[33] "River Jayhun (Oxus) is also known as the Amuyah, and its (head waters) are formed by the junction of six streams. It is a very famous river, and it forms the eastern boundary of Iran, flowing from south to north. One of its head streams comes down from the mountains of Tibet, another is from the hills of Badakhshan, a third from the Saghaniyan frontiers, and a fourth is from the limits of Khutlan. Each one of these, prior to its junction with the main river receives many minor streams, and certain of these have their courses through the lands of Balkh and Tirmid. After all these streams have come together, the Oxus passes through the Narrows, which are known as the Defile of the Lion's Mouth. This is near the village of Buqshah, which is a dependency of Hazarasp. This defile runs between two mountains, which approach so near one to the other that the space in between is barely 100 ells across. The water rushes through with a mighty roar, and then is lost underground in the sands. Here for the space of a league it is no longer visible; and there is no possibility of crossing the sands above. (When the stream has come again to view) many great canals are led off from the Oxus, beside which stand mighty towns and many cultivated lands. Of such are the

Canal of Gav Khuwarah, the Hazarasp Stream, that of Karduran Khas, the Karih Canal, the Khivah Canal and others, and in each of them boats can with ease pass along. Some of these canals have their outflow to the Khwarazm Lake (the Aral), but the main stream of the Oxus after passing the city of Khwarazm flows down the Halam gorge, which in Turki is called Kurladi. Here at a league's distance, or even three leagues away, you may hear the rushing of the waters. Finally the Oxus flows out to the Sea of Khazar (the Caspian), at a place called Khalkhal, which is a fishing station; and from the city of Khwarazm to its month in the Caspian is a distance of six days' march. The whole length of the Oxus is 500 leagues. In winter time the water is so fast frozen that in many places, caravans can cross on the surface of the ice. The wells there descend to a depth of several ells, in order to get to water."

Babur crossed once Amu at a place called Aubaj-ferry. On various occasions he remained on the bank of Amu which could be crossed with ford, if water rose, fords changed. There was a Persian proverb, "The waters have carried down the fords."[34]

Elsewhere the Oxus has been mentioned as the largest river of Soviet Central Asia originating in the Hindukush and Pamir mountain ranges, which extends 1578 miles to the Aral Sea. Two-thirds of the flow is concentrated in the period from May to August, the result of melting from the glaciers and perennial snow -fields of the high mountains. The Oxus forms part of the boundary between Afghanistan and the former USSR and divides the desert of the Kara Kum and Kizil Kum in the Turan Lowlands.[35]

About river Syr Al-Muqaddassi states, "The river al-Shash (Syr Darya) emerges from the right of the country of the Turks (Turkistan) and flows also into the lake of Khwarizm (Aral Sea). It approaches the Jayhun River in volume, but it appears, as it were, without life. Then a channel runs from it into the area lying between Usrushana and Ghujanda. From the beginning to the end.[36]

In *Hudud al-Alam* it has been mentioned as river PARAK which rises from behind the Khallukh mountains and takes a southern direction, flowing through the limits of Chach. Between Banakat and the wall of Qalas it joins the Uzkand. When all rivers had united, their joint course was called the CHAC RIVER and the Arabs called it Sayhun.[37]

Chang Chun a medieval Chinese traveller crossed this river on a floating bridge, and stopped on its western bank. He mentions Syr as river Ho-chan-mu-lien. Mu-lilen here is intended for "muren"or river in Mongol. Ho-chian means the river of Khodjand or the Jaxartes of the Greek, the Sihun of the Arabian geographers of the Middle Ages, known also under the name of river of Shash (Tashkand).[38] Friar John of Pian de Carpine also mentions the river but does not know the name, but it was certainly the Syr.[39] Hamdullah Mustawfi calls it river Sayhun which was of Ma-war a-n-Nahr because to the west of it flew the Oxus, while to the east of it flew the Jaxartes and thus from either it was regarded as the Land beyond the river. The country called the Jaxartes by the name Gul Zaryun. It rose among the snows, then its stream passed Khujand and Fanakat and finally reached the Khwarizm Lake (Aral). This river too, like the Oxus, freezed so hard in winter that at many places caravan crossed on the snow. The length of the river was 80 leagues.[40]

The other significiant, river of the region is Zarafshan Darya (Gold-rolling river) which rises in a long glacier of that name (old name Sugd) in the east-west Alay range, the first rampart of the Pamir Plateau and disappears in the Kyzlkum desert in Kazakhstan. The Kashka Darya on its right southern bank is one of its great tributaries. The valley of the Zarafshan Darya is the heartland of West Central Asia. The Chu Darya rises in the Tien Shan range and disappears in the sands of the desert Muiumkum. The Atrak (river of the Turks) Darya is West Asia's only river, which flows into the Caspian Sea. The Turks lived on its bank in the ancient time. It rises near Nisa, west of Ashkabat, Turkmenistan and is very deep. The

Murgab and Tejen do not reach the Caspian Sea. The Murgab disappears in the sand, west of Merv.[41]

Deserts

Among the deserts of the region are the Karakum (Black Sand) Desert in Turkmenistan and Kyzylkum (Red Sand) Desert in Kazakhstan of West Central Asia. These are separated by Amu Darya. The Karakum Desert, located to the west of the Amu Darya and bounded in the north by the ust-yurt plateau, to the Caspian Sea and taken up the entire middle part of Turkmenistan. The Kyzylkum located between the Amu Darya and Syr Darya, has no sand deposits.[42]

In the ancient times the Chinese knew the entire region west of Changan, the capital of China then as Xiyu (western region). The Chaghatai period knew it as Mongolistan (Mongol land). Since then it has been the eastern part of what the Moroccan traveller Ibn Batutta (1304-08) called it Turkistan (land of the Turks). Most of it is the great desert of the region, located in the central basin of the Tarim Darya and its tributaries flowing along it from west to east. The highest peaks of Xinjiang are in the Karakoram, Kunlum and Tianshan ranges. The Tianshan range is an extensive mountain system, branching east-north-east from the Panir Knot. It divides Xinjing into two parts north and south. North is smaller than the south. The Ili river north of Tienshan range and the Tarim river south of it are the principal rivers of Xinjiang. The Ili flows north into Lake Balkhash in East Kazakhstan and provided water resources of the Ili valley. The Tarim Darya flows through the Tarim town, south of Kucha; hence its name The Aksu, Kashghar, Yarkand, Yarhad, Khotan, Kenija rivers, which rise in the Tienshan, Karakorum and Kunlun rages, either disappear in the great descent or flow into the Tarim Darya, their joint water. The Kashghar Darya which rises in the Altai range and which is the location of the city of Kashghar, loses itself in the sands of the Tokrakun Desert. It does not join the Tarim Darya.

The Yarkand Darya, which rises in the Karakoram ranges in the south west as the Raskam Darya, is the most important tributary of the Tarim Darya. The Tashkurgan Darya, which rises in the south west is also an important tributary of the Tarim Darya. The Khotan Darya at Silin, the Tarim which flows east into the great lake Lob Nor in the Gobi, which means 'desert' is the main river of south Xinjiang and its lifeline.[43]

Due to its distinct eclogical features, Central Asia has played two important, and in some ways contradictory functions, in the history of mankind. On the one hand, as a result of its enormous extent, prevailing aridity and the absence of natural means of communication (most of its major river systems flow north into the Arctic Ocean) its principal functions have been to keep apart the civilizations which prosper on its peripheries—Chinese, Indian, Iranian, Russian etc. On the other hand, its ancient caravan-route provided a slender but almost unbroken thread by means of which those same peripheral civilizations acquired a limited knowledge of their neighbours in addition to exchange valuable commodities which might otherwise have been in accessible or at least more difficult to obtain.

References

1. *The New Encyclopaedia of Britannica,* vol. 15, (1999], p. 701. *Encyclopaedia of Asian History,* Vol. I. Ed. Ainslie T. Embree London, 1988 (p. 239) reads that Central Asia is composed of the Xinjiang, Uighur Autonomous Region (in China), the territory north of Hindukush in Afghanistan and the Uzbek, Kazakh, Kirghiz, Turkmen and Tajik Soviet Socialist Republics.
2. Ibid., p. 706
3. Ram Rahul, *Central Asia: An Outline History* (New Delhi], 1997, p.11.
4. Gavin Hambly and others(Ed.) *Central Asia* (London, 1969], p. xi.
5. K. Warikoo and David Norber (Ed.) *Ethnicity and Politics in Central Asia* (New Delhi 1992], p. viii.
6. Ahmad Hasan Dani, *New Light on Central Asia,* (Delhi, 1993], p. 9

7. Ibid. pp. 30-31
8. Ibid. p.57
9. Yuriv Kulchik, Abndrey Fadin and Victor Sergeev, *Central Asia after the Empire* (London, 1996], p. 1.
10. *Qaidu and the Rise of the Independent Mongol State,* p. 132, note 11.
11. *Mongol, Turks and Others,* p. 201. A good discussion has been done by Scott C. Levi in his *The Indian diaspora in Central Asia and its Trade,* 1550-1900 (Brill, 2002), pp. 8-12.
12. Edgar Knobloch, *Beyond the Oxus,* p. 9.
13. Ibid, p. 25.
14. Ram Rahul, *March of Central Asia* (New Delhi, 2002], p. 17.
15. Marco Polo, *The Travels of Marco Polo,* English translation by Ronald Latham (Penguin, Books, 1959], p. 49.
16. *The Journey of William of Rubruck,* p. 161.
17. *Medieval Researches,* i, p. 80.
18. Gibb, iii, p. 586.
19. *Beyond the Oxus,* p. 16.
20. Hambly Gavin, op.cit., p. 4.
21. *Lands of the Eastern Caliphate,* pp. 433-45.
22. Regarding the origin of the name Khwarizm, Al-Muqaddassi narrates a very interesting anecdote. "It is said that in olden times the king of al-Mashriq grew angry with four hundred men of his kingdom, especially at his court, and he ordered them to be taken to a place removed from civilization, so that they would be a hundred *farsakhs* removed; and this happened to be about the location of Kath. After a considerable period of time he sent some people who would present him with a report on them; and when they arrived there, they found them alive, having built huts for themselves, and they saw them fishing for their sustenance; here also was plenty of firewood. When they returned to the king and told him about this said he, "what name do they call 'meat'?" Said they, "Khwar". "And firewood?" Said they, "Razm." Said the king, "I have caused them to settle in that area, so I name it Khwarzam". Moreover, he ordered four hundred Turkish maidens to be brought to them, so that to this day there remains among them rememblance to the Turks". See Al-Muqaddassi, pp 252-53.
23. *Hudud al-Alam,* p. 71.
24. S. Maqbul Ahmad and A. Rahman (Ed.) *Al-Masudi: Millenary Commemoration Volume* (Aligarh, 1960), p. 75. For more details, see Al-Muqaddassi, pp. 258-59 and *The Lands of the Eastern Caliphate,* p. 433.
25. *Medieval Researches,* i, p. 22.
26. Ibid, p. 77. Al Muqaddassi identifies at least twenty five crossing points of the river Amu and lists the branches of the river: Nahr Hazarasp, Nahr Kardaran Khas, Nahr Khiwah, Nahr Wadak, Nahr Madra, Nahr Buwwah and Nahr Kurdar. See Al Muqaddassi, p. 259.

27. *Medieval Researches,* pp. 85, 92 and 94. Halaku Khan crossed the Amu on 2nd of January 1256 (p. 115). Changte crossed it on April 7, 1256 (p. 132).
28. *Lata' if al-ma' arif,* p. 143.
29. *History of the World Conqueror,* p. 147. Compare with the account of Carpini who mentions the fear of Quour for horses *Journey of the Friar William,* p. 4.
30. Ahmad Ibn Arabshah, op.cit, pp. 7-8.
31. *Muqaddimah,* I, pp.102-3.
32. Ibid. p. 18-19.
33. *Nuzhat-al-Qulub,* pp. 205-6.
34. *Baburnama,* pp. 193, 189, 249. Thackston reads "The water carried off the crossing," p. 165.
35. *Encyclopedia of Asian History,* Volume 3, p. 167.
36. *Al-Muqaddassi,* pp. 23-24.
37. *Hudud al-Alam,* p. 73.
38. *Medieval Researches,* i, p. 75 and note 189.
39. *The Journey of William of Rubruck,* p. 14.
40. *Nuzhat–al-Qulub,* pp. 209-10.
41. Ram Rahul, *March of Central Asia,* p.18.
42. Svat Soucek, *A History of Inner Asia,* p. 4.
43. *March of Central Asia,* pp. 14-15.

2

Rise of the Mongols

THE MONGOL EMPIRE OF THE thirteenth and fourteenth centuries was vast—it extended what is today Korea to Hungary, encompassed the entire Asian continent up to India, South-east Asia and Eastern Europe. It existed in this size for more than a hundred years and in some regions for even longer as partial or successive empire. The main difference between the Mongols and earlier conquerors is that no other previous nomad empire has controlled the Asian inner steppe and vast regions of settled peoples.[1]

Nomadic pastoralist societies had developed wherever peasant agriculture did not find the terrain or the political resources to establish or maintain itself. The pastoralist society of the Eurasian steppes was built on a vaster scale and was more complexly related to agrarian societies. The steppes were on the whole better watered and the steppe nomads made greater use of horses than of camels, and were perhaps more self-contained.

Early in the thirteenth century, a new formation arose under their leader Chingiz Khan who unified most of the steppe nomads and conquered the urban trading centers of Inner Asia. Drawing upon this population of herders and townsmen, he organized a powerful state that served as a foundation for the even greater empire carved out by his heirs. All of the major civilizations at this time were in a state of political fragmentations and were vulnerable to attacks from across their frontiers. The Mongols were able to gain control over frontier regions of several 'civilized' societies simultaneously and by utilizing the resources obtained thereby, continued their expansion until whole civilizations were brought under their rule.[2]

About the home and conditions of the Mongols Juvaini hints at an immense valley, whose area was a journey of seven or eight months both in length and breadth in those days. In the east it went up to the land of Khitai (Northern China), in the west the country of the Uighur (settled in the various oases to the north of the Tarim], in the north the Qirghiz and river Selengie and in the south the Tangut (they were a people of Tibetan origin who had founded a kingdom in North-Western China) and the Tibetans. Before the appearance of Chingiz Khan, they had no chief or ruler. Each tribe or two tribes lived separately; they were not united with one another, and there was constant fighting and hostility between them. Some of them regarded robbery and violence, immorality and debauchery (*fisq va fujur*) as deeds of manliness and excellence. The Khan of Khitai used to demand and seize goods from them. Their clothing was of the skins of dogs and mice, and their food was the flesh of those animals and other dead things; their wine was mares' milk and their desert the fruit of a tree shaped like the pine, which they call *qusuq*. . . .[3]

Minhaj denounces them by talks of the depravity, robbery and adultery, greatly prevailed; and both in their words and deeds, save lying, inequity, robbery and adultery, naught went on.[4] The main sources of livelihood for the steppe-dwellers were cattle-breeding, horse breeding, hunting and fishing.[5] Agriculture was almost unknown to them. *Yuan-Chao-Pi-shi (Secret History of the Mongols)*, the only extant authority on the early career of Chingiz Khan makes no reference to any cultivated field or farmer. Basically Mongolia, the land of the Mongols was of striking contrasts, of "lofty mountains with snow-lopped peaks and rich, wooded areas with rivers, streams and lakes."[6]

It is hemmed in by mountain in the east, the west and the north that blocks precipitation and in the south, the Gobi Desert offers a formidable obstacle. Most of the Gobi is suitable neither for a pastoral nor an agricultural economy. Though it is not entirely lifeless, its almost unbearable heat in summer and chilling winds and patches of snow in winter make it most inhospitable. Only the sturdiest of humans and animals can survive in this bleak and hostile environment. The traditional economy relied upon five principal animals—sheep, goats and yaks for food, clothing, shelter and fuel, camels for transport, thus facilitating trade participatory through the deserts; and horses for mobility. Horses were used in cavalries in warfare and provided the mainstays of the justly renowned Mongol postal system, which enabled them to transmit official messages and reports throughout their domains. In the beginning of the twelfth century, three important tribes dominated the area now known as Mongolia. In the extreme east around the Buir-Nor and Kulun - Nor were the Tatars. West of them in the country watered by the rivers Tola, Orkhon, upper Onon and Kerulen were the Karaits. Further to the west, between the Selenga river and the Altai were the Naimans. The Mongols themselves grazed their flocks and herds beside the Onon and Kerulen rivers between the pastures of the Karaits and the Tatars. North of the Karaits and the Naimans were other tribes of which the most important were the Oriots and the Merkits.[7]

Stanley Lane-Poole has given comments on the early history of the Mongols. He writes: "The history of the Mongols begins practically with the great conqueror Chingiz Khan. There are many traditions of his ancestors current among his biographers, but, as in the case of many other men of unexpected fame, his pedigree has been elaborated rather on the ground of natural propriety than of fact. All that can safely be said about the early history of the Mongols is that they were a clan among clans, a member of a great nomad confederacy that ravaged the country north of the desert of Gobi in search of water and pasture; who spent their lives in hunting and the breeding of cattle, lived on flesh and sour milk (kumis], and made their profit by bartering hides and beasts with their kinsmen the Khitans, or with the Turks and Chinese, to whom they owed allegiance. The name Mongol was not known abroad until the tenth century, and probably came to be applied to the whole group of clans only when the chief of a particular class bearing that name acquired an ascendancy over the rest of the confederacy, and gave to the greater the name of the less. If not the founder of the supremacy of his clan, Yissugay was a notable maintainer of it, and it was probably he who first asserted the independence of the Mongols from Chinese rule. In spite, however, of conquest and annexation, the people who owned the sovereignty of Yissugay numbered only forty thousand tents. Yet it was upon this foundation that Yissugay's son Chingiz Khan, built up in twenty years the widest empire the world has ever seen."[8]

Most of the inhabitants of Mongolia were Shamanists, although it was only among the forest-dwellers that the shaman exercised a dominant influence over tribal affairs. On the steppes leadership was invested in tribal and clan chieftainship whose status and functions gave society a distinctly secular and aristocratic character. Tribal chieftains were called *khans* and the ruler of a tribal confederacy took the title of *Khaqan.* Away from the forests economic life was pastoral nomadic, the prosperity and capacity for survival of a tribe depending upon the quality and extent of the pastures to which it had access. Among more advanced tribes trade played a subsidiary but not unimportant part in the economy.[9]

Many theories have been forwarded by the scholars for the rise of the Mongols as the world power. One of the explanation has been suggested that any pastoral society like that of the Mongols, who were fully nomadic, was bound to suffer chronic economic instability. The lack of self sufficiency in grain and weapons was a constant incentive for expansion toward settled areas of supply. In the military technology of the day, moreover, cavalry had become the dominant weapon, a ready means of conquest possessed by the Mongols. To catalyze these elements a dynamic centralization of political authority among the tribes of the steppe under a leader of genius had to coincide with a period of dis-organization and weakness among the sedentary societies on the periphery.[10]

Minhaj, a Persian chronicler of the thirteenth century on the belief that world would become to an end in the year 610, but since it could not, he mentions Muhammad Ghuri's assassination as the first of those signs which happened in 602 H and in the same year Chinghiz Khan, the Mongol rose up in the kingdom of China and Tamghaj (Turkistan].[11]

In European writings also the same myth was current which has been expressed in a different way in these words: "It is believed that these Tartars, of cursed memory, are of the ten tribes who having forsaken the Mosaic Law, followed after the golden calves, and whom Alexander the Macedonian endeavoured at first to shut up in the rugged mountains of the Caspian with bitumen-covered rocks. When he saw that the undertaking exceeded the power of man, he invokved the might of the God of Israel, and the tops of the mountains came together, and an inaccessible and impassable place was made. Josephus says of this place "will God do as much for the believer as he has done for the unbeliever?" So it seemed that God did not wish them to come out; nevertheless, it is written in sacred history that they shall come out toward the end of the world, and shall make a great slaughter of men. There arises, however, a doubt whether the Tartars now coming from there be really they, for they do not use the Hebrew tongue, neither do they know the laws of Moses, nor have they laws, nor are they governed by them. To which it may be answered that notwithstanding this, it is credible that they may belong to those who were shut up, and whom reference has been made . . . .[12]

China had already been divided for a century between those dubbed as Sino-barbarian dynasty of the Chin and the unwarlike southern Sung. On the northwest frontier of China in modern Kansu was the Hsi Hsia kingdom of the Tanguts. Further west were the Uighur Turks, who had settled down in small oasis states of Central Asia, like that of Turfan and were no longer the military power they had been in the Tang period. The Arab—Turkish society of the Middle East similarly was in military decay five hundred years after the Arab conquest of those reigns. It included the empire of Khwarizm which had reached the height of its power on the Amu Darya, south of the Aral Sea, Abbassid Caliphate at Baghdad and many smaller states. Against these disunited, semi or fully agrarian and commercial states all across Asia, the Mongols brought to bear an invincible military power. They were organized for conquest and they succeeded both in conquering and in administrating vast areas. When Chingiz Khan, the creator of the Mongol empire was born, the Mongolian-speaking tribes still lacked a common name. Some were composed of hunters and fishermen living in small groups on the fringe of the Siberian forest. Interestingly the Mongols had long since taken up a life on horseback on the open steppe, and lived in small groups, each family in its felt tent or *yurt.* At the times of seasonable migration these scattered units might form larger groups of several hundred *yurts.*[13]

The basic social and political units were patriarchal clans. The individual's spiritual life was focused on loyalty to his clan, which was expressed in a cult of the hearth. Since a group of clans, bound together by their blood relationships, formed a larger tribal unit, the individual felt a similar loyalty to his tribe. Within this social framework, one Mongol might choose to become a "sworn brother" of another by a personal alliance between the two of them as members of different clans; adoption was also practiced in this society which remained rather open and fluid. The traditional institutions of polygamy heightened the demand for wives, but these had to be acquired from outside the clan because marriage was considered impossible within a clan or even between members of closely related clans. Consequently, wives were often acquired by seizure, a practice, which naturally fostered feuds, raids of vengeance and petty warfare between clans or even whole tribes. As a result of tribal warfare, clan groups of families would become subordinate to other tribes, enhancing their power. Chinghiz enters history chiefly as an organizer and unifier of the Mongol tribes.[14]

There are many anecdotes regarding the birth of Chingiz Khan. In the *Secret History of the Mongols* it is mentioned that Chingiz was born clutching in his right hand a clot of blood the size of a knucklebone. Because he was born when the Tatar Temujin Uge had been brought captive, for this very reason they gave him the name Temujin. The source further claims that when Temujin was nine years old, his father, Yesugai took him to maternal uncles for a girl in marriage for him. On the way he met one Dei Secen who said, this boy of yours is a boy :

Who has fires in his eyes
Who has light in his face

Dei Secen had seen his dream that a white gerfalcon clasping both sun and moon in its claws flew to him and perched on his head. Since this dream was on the occasion of Temujin visiting his uncles, Dei Secen took it a good omen and offered his daughter Borte in marriage, one year older than Temujin. Temujin was left with Dei Secen as his son-in-law. On the way back Yesugei was poisoned by his enemies.[15]

According to Minhaj, Chingiz Khan had become noted and famous among the fraternity for his manhood, vigour, valour and intrepidity, all concurred in naming him for the chieftainship (saying]: "For, save him, no one will be capable to undertake the carrying out of these matters, and this affair will not be accomplished, nor succeed at the hands of any other except him". He further writes, "Chinghiz Khan bound the whole of the people of the tribes by pledges and oaths to obey him in all things, and submit to his command; and, in conformity with the usual customs in force among that people, these important matters were caused to be ratified. He said: "If you will be obedient to my mandates, it behoveth that, if I should command the sons to slay the fathers, you should all obey" and they entered into a solemn promise accordingly."[16]

He was of aristocratic birth but lived in humble circumstances in his youth. He rose slowly, and after reaching maturity was still merely the vassal of a minor chieftain. Before he could build up a personal following, Temujin had to master the complicated art of tribal politics, which required a creative mixture of loyalty, rivalry, cunning and ruthless treachery, as well as physical prowess. Rebelling against his overload, he subjugated the Kereit tribe and the Niaman and others. Finally, at the great meeting of the Mongol tribes' the *quriltai* of 1206 on the Kerulen River, he was confirmed to the title of Chingiz Khan which seems to have had some connotation of "universal ruler". At that time, the chieftains of all the Mongol tribes committed themselves to his leadership.[17] In *Erdeni Tunumal Sudur* ("The Jewel Translucent Sutra"), a recently discovered biography of Altan Khan written after more than two hundred year of the Mongol rule, a brief history of Mongol rulers and their legitimacy is outlined in the introduction of the book in these words:

"Born by the fate of the Supreme Tengri,
From its beginning creating the supreme State,

(Temujin) caused all those of the world to enter into his power. Temujin became famous as the Great Chingiz Khan."[18]

Secret History of the Mongols gives a list of ninety-five commanders who were given the rank of one thousand and assigned them with their duties with different offices.[19] However, Minhaj tells that the number of the Mongols had largely increased and become very large.[20]

From some accounts, which have come down to us written for the most part long afterwards by Persian, Chinese, Arabian chroniclers on the basis of oral legends, we can see some of Chingiz Khan's methods of organization. To secure a religious sanction, he asserted his own divine mission, delegated to heir by the External Heaven, the deity of the steppe. The political structure he built up was organized on the family principle, families forming clan, clans forming tribes, tribes grouped in larger units and the latter forming an empire.[21]

As a permanent basis of rule, superior to Khan himself, he drew up an imperial code of laws called *Yasa* and made it supreme over his people. Juvaini explains that Chingiz Khan invented these from the page of his own mind. "And indeed, Alexander who was so addicted to the devising of talisman and the solving of enigmas, had he lived in the age of Chingiz Khan would have been his pupil in craft and cunning." . . . [22]

The extreme example of Chinghiz Khan's disciplinary mandate on one occasion against Altun Khan, the king of upper Turkistan, we find a Herculean example in Minhaj's account who writes "He enjoined that all the men should be separated from the women, and the children from their mothers: and, for three whole days and nights, all of them remained bare headed; and for three days no one tasted food, and no animal was allowed to give milk to its young. Chinghiz Khan himself entered a *Khargah* (a felt tent], and placed a tent-rope around his neck, and came not forth from it for three nights and days; and during this period, the whole of the people were crying out, Tingri! Tingri!" After three days Chinghiz Khan broke the silence and went against his enemy.[23] Minhaj further relates "Chinghiz Khan continued before the city (Altun Khan's seat of government) for a period of four years, in such wise that every stone which was in that city they (the defenders) used to place in the catapults and discharge against the investors; and when stones, bricks, and the like, ceased to be available, everything that was of iron, brass, lead, copper, tin, and pewter, all was expanded in the catapults, and then balishts (ingots) of gold and silver they continued to discharge in place of stones. Trustworthy (persons) have narrated on this wise, that the Chingiz Khan, during this period, had issued a mandate that no person in the Mughal army should take any notice of that gold and silver, nor remove any of it from the place where it might have fallen." Interestingly, when he acquired a copy of the records of the treasuries of Altun Khan and number of gold and silver *balishts* were discharged, not a single bare thereof was missing.[24]

The Great *Yasa* was first promulgated in 1204 and further development during the remaining twenty years before he died in 1227. It formulated, no doubt, from customary sources, the basic rules of organization for the imperial family and regime, and for the Mongol nation, the army and the administration and also laid down criminal, civil and commercial laws. Chingiz in 1204 had acquired the services of an 'Uighur Guardian of the Seals' and in 1215, he brought away with him from Peking a Kitan advisor Yeh-lu Ch'u-tsai thereby inaugurating the Mongol policy of employing foreign advisers, often eminent men of barbarian origin. This common law was buttressed by heavy penalties; the penalty for murder, serious theft, false pretences, adultery, was death.[25]

Military organization was, of course, the first secret of success. Chingiz's personal body guard as early as 1203 posted eighty men around his tent by night. Eventually his guard grew to an elite corps of 10000, recruited from the sons of clan leaders, generals and kinsmen, many if not most of them known personally to Chingiz. The guard members were kept under fierce discipline. They were beaten if they did not arrive promptly for duty and they stood watch for three days and nights at a time. In return they enjoyed a high status and many privileges. A private of the guard rated above an army captain of 1000.

From this elite group, Chingiz chose his generals and top administrators, some at the age of twenty. Under them the army was organized on a decimal system in units of tens, hundreds and thousands, usually with clan members carefully intermixed. The whole force at the time of his death in 1227 amounted to about 129,000 men, a huge army by nomad standards but small as compared with those of China. Even at the height of his campaigns, he probably never had more than 250,000 men under his command, many drawn from the non-Chinese (especially Turkish) allies of the Mongols. The total population of the Mongols could not have succeeded 2,500,000 and perhaps was closer to 1,000,000 at that time.

The Mongol war machine was the climax of a long development. Its success lay first of all in the quality of its individual warriors and in their coordination with one another. The Mongol cavalry had been trained in the saddle from boyhood as scouts and hunters. They fought under hereditary, aristocratic leaders who maintained personal control and discipline. Clad in leather and furs, leading extra horses as remounts and capable of living in the saddle as long as ten days and nights at a time, those troops cover distances which seemed incredible to the world of thirteenth century. They were said to have once covered 270 miles during three days in Hungary. They could live on mares' milk or even, so it is said, on the blood of their horses. They carried leather bags for water, which when empty could be inflated to help them in swimming streams. Their herds followed them, but the troops lived mainly on the plunder.[26]

The European writers depict the Mongols as treacherous and cruel. "That the joys of mortal men be not enduring, nor worldly happiness long lasting without lamentations, in this same year (i.e. 1240) a detestable nation of Satabn, to wit, the countless army of the Tartars, broke loose from its mountain-environed home, and piercing the solid rocks (of the Caucasus], poured forth like devils from the Tartarus, so that they are rightly called Tartari or Tartarians. Swarming like locusts over the face of the earth, they have brought terrible devastation to the eastern parts (of Europe), laying it waste with fire and carnage. After having passed through the land of the Saracens, they have razed cities, cut down forests, overthrown fortresses, pulled up vines, destroyed gardens, killed townspeople and peasants. If perchance they have spared any suppliants, they have forced them, reduced to the lowest condition of slavery, to fight in the foremost ranks against their own neighbours. Those who have feigned to fight, or have hidden in the hope of escaping, have been followed up by the Tartars and butchered. If any have fought bravely (for them) and conquered, they have got no thanks for reward; and so they have misused their captives as they have their mares. For they are inhuman and beastly, rather monsters than men, thirsting for and drinking blood, tearing and devouring the flesh of dogs and men, dressed in ox-hides, armed with plates of iron, short and stout, thickset, strong, invincible, indefatigable, their backs unprotected, their breasts covered with armour; drinking with delight the pure blood of their flocks, with big, strong horses, which eat branches and even trees, and which they have to mount by the help of three steps on account of the shortness of their things. They are without human laws, know no comforts, are more ferocious than lions or bears, have boats made of ox-hides, which ten or twelve of them own in common; they are able to swim or to manage a boat, so that they can cross the largest and swiftest rivers without let or hindrance, drinking turbid or muddy water when blood fails them (as beverage). They have one-edged swords and daggers, are wonderful archers, spare neither age, nor sex, nor condition. They know no other language than their own, which no one else knows; for until now there has been no access to them, nor did they go forth (from their own country); so there could be no knowledge of their customs or persons through the common intercourse of men. They wander about with their flocks and their wives, who are taught to fight like men. And so they came with the swiftness of lightning to the confines of Christendom, ravaging and slaughtering, striking every one with terror and incomparable horror. It was for this that the Saracens sought to ally themselves with the Christians, hoping to be able to resist these monsters with their combined forces."[27]

The account of Friar John of Pian de Carpine reveals that the horses which his team had during their journey towards Mongolia were to leave behind at Kiev, as the animals died due to the deep snow on the way and they did not know how to dig out the grass from under the snow like Tartar horses, nor could anything else be found (on the way) for them to eat, for the Tartars had neither straw nor hay nor fodder.[28]

About the war strategy followed by the Mongols the best example we find in the *Secret History of the Mongols* where we see Chinghiz Khan instructing and ordering Subetai, one of his great generals, who had been provided with an iron cart, to pursue the sons of Toqto'a headed by Qudu, Qal and Cila'un. When he sent him on his mission Chingiz said, "The sons of Toqoto'a having at their head Qudu, Qal and Cila'un left in flight and haste, then turned back, exchanged shots with us and went off like lassoed wild asses or stages with arrows in their bodies. If they grow wings and fly up into the sky, you, Subetei, will you not fly up like a gerfalcon and catch them? If they turn into marmots and burrow into the ground with their claws, will you not become an iron rod and, digging and searching for them, catch up them? If they turn into fish and plung into the Tenggis Sea (the Ocean) you Subeetei, will you not become a casting net and a dragnet and get them by scooping them out? And again, I send you cross the mountain passes to ford wide rivers; mindful of the long distance you have to cover, you must spare the army mounts before they become to lean and you must save your provisions before they come to an end. If a gelding is already completely exhausted it will be of no use to spare it then; if your provisions have already completely run out, how can you save them? There will be many wild animals on way: when you go, thinking ahead, do not allow your soldiers to gallop after and hunt down wild animals, nor let them make circular battles without limit. If you make a battle i.e. a hunt in which the game is driven towards a central point, in order to give additional provisions to your troops, hunt with moderation. Except on limited battles, do not allow the soldiers to fix the crupper to the saddle and put on the bridle, but let the horses go with their mouths free (Lit. removing the bit from the mouth, so that it hung free). If they so discipline themselves, the soldiers will not be able to gallop on the way. Thus, making this a matter of law, whoever than transgresses it (Lit. the law—*jasaq*) shall be seized and beaten. Send to Us those transgress our order if it looks that they are personally know to us; as for the many who are not known to us, just cut them down on the spot.

Beyond the rivers
You will perhaps lose courage,
But continue to advance
In the same way;
Beyond the mountains
You mission will perhaps lose heart,
But think of nothing else apart from your mission.

He further gave final instructions: "If you constantly think that even though we are out of sight it is as if We were visible, and even though We are far it is as if We were near you will also be protected by Heaven Above!"[29]

The other tactics included flying horse columns, carrying of heavy and light bows with armour-piercing arrows to surround the enemies on false chasing, using colour pennants or lanterns, smoke signals and messengers having horses of a separate colour. All these devices increased mobility and coordination through which crushing force could be concentrated against the opponents' weak points. The Mongol thus brought offensive power to its highest points in the age before the development of firearms. Even against walled fortresses they soon mastered the medieval art of seize warfare. The Mongols were also masters of espionage and psychological warfare. Spies were ready at hand among the merchants on the trade routes, so that the Mongols had little difficult in learning what they wanted to know about their victims. By putting whole cities to the sword, they let terror run ahead of them as a weapon in itself. Many ancient centers of culture were all but wiped out, the women and children enslaved, the men forced to be the frontline of assault on the next city. To capitalize on this terrorism, they also spread fair promises of toleration for religious minorities and freedom for merchants and the oppressed, providing they all surrendered without delay.[30]

Thus imposing tight discipline on his troops, developing an intelligence network, establishing an excellent cavalry and devising new tactics and adopting traditional ones such as the feigned retreats planned his campaign thoroughly. With the powerful force that he had created, and through the judicious use of alliance, he succeeded in subduing the Tatars, the Kereyid, the Naimans, the Merkid and the other leading tribes in the Mongol terrirotires. Having pacified the Mongols and other tribes Chingiz sought to bring other lands under his control. Before an attack on another state, he invariably sent envoys to the foreign ruler with so-called orders of submission, demanding acquiescence to his rule. Often, if the foreign state agreed he would allow its leaders to retain power, so long as they offered taxes and performed the services he required, but if refused to submit, he was ruthless in overcoming it resistance.[31]

The same views also have been brought forward by modern scholars that the native dynasties were allowed to retain their thrones and territories as subjects of the *Khaqan* for a variety of reasons. In some instances, distance (e.g. Bulgaria), inaccessibility (e.g. Kashmir), or climatic conditions (e.g. Burma) made the military efforts necessary to force capitulation very costly. In order to avoid such campaigns, the Mongols, prior to the commencement of hostilities, customarily issued orders of submission that in essence offered local rulers physical and institutional survival in return for submission to the *Khaqan*. The choice given potential vassals in graphically expressed in a *jarligh* issued in the name of the Grand Khan Mongke (1251-59) that his brother Hulegu caused to be sent to the ruling houses of the Middle East on the eve of the Mongol campaign against the Assassins:

> "If you come of your own accord and support our army with men and supplies, your countries, armies and households will remain with you and your efforts on our (behalf) will be looked upon with favor. But, if you are negligent and cultivate remissness in carrying out the orders then as soon as we, with God's power, finish with them (the Assassins], we, without fail, will head in your direction and deal with your households and countries in the same manner we dealt with them."[32]

It is further suggested, "such offers were also a valuable diplomatic tool for weakening the resolve of an enemy and a means of detaching his subordinates and allies. Despite Chinggis Khan's injunction, reported in the *Tartar Relation*, that the Mongols should "make peace with none unless they surrendered unconditionally and without treaty," his successors retained a degree of flexibility in dealing with foreign states that proved useful for diplomatic purposes. For example, Mongol granted Hetum, the king of Lesser Armenia, certain concessions which were formalized by treaty, in order to gaint he latter's support for the attack on Baghdad.

"Another and perhaps more compelling reason for the toleration of dependent states was the Mongols' lack of experienced administrative manpower. Since very few of the Mongols' estimated population of 700,000 were literate, and still fewer were familiar with the "customs and laws of cities", the retention of a local dynasty and its attendant administrative apparatus was often the most practical method of controlling and exploiting the population and resources of a newly surrendered territory. In several instances, the Mongols even created new dynasties—for example, the Kart of Herat, headed by a family familiar with local languages, conditions and administrative practices. Similarly, the Sa-skya, the Lamaist sect that ruled Tibet in the thirteenth and fourteenth centuries, was also a creation of the Mongols.

"Among the vassals of the Mongols, the Uighurs, as Rubruck correctly notes, "were the first dwellers in towns to be subject to Chingis Chan. Because of their early adherence to the empire, as well as their proximity to the Mongol homeland and their administrative and clerical skills, the Uighurs had a close and continuous relationship with the Mongol Grand Khans for nearly a hundred year."[33]

Certain psychological factors made the task of empire-building progressively less formidable. Success breech success and the desire for plunder among the Mongol troops was reinforced by a courage and determination derived from confidence in their commanders and only in Chinghiz Khan himself. Several sons and grandsons, as well as his favourable paladins inspired equal trust and remained remarkably loyal to the ideal of imperial unity. The opponents of the Mongols, divided among themselves, ignorant of their adversaries, demoralized by deceit, bribery and a deliberate policy of terror, were rarely capable of prolonged resistance.[34]

His military campaigns were remarkably successful. First he compelled His Hsia-dynasty of Northwest China, founded by the Tanguts, to offer tribute. Then, with control of China's trade routes through the Northwest, he turned his attentions to North China, then governed by the Jurchens, who had founded the Chin dynasty. By 1215, his troops had captured the Chin capital of Yen-Ching (Peking), forcing the royal family to flee south to Kai-feng, where for almost two decades they staved off a final defeat. In 1219, turning westward, Chingiz led two hundred thousand troops on a punitive expedition in Central Asia against the Khwarizmian Shah Alauddin Muhammad, who had executed several of the Khan's merchants and envoys. The details of the campaigns against Khwrarizm have been given in all Persian Chronicles, which have been discussed by modern scholars. By February of 1220, Mongol troops had sacked the Central Asian town of Bukhara and within a month they occupied and looted Samarkand, massacring many of its inhabitants but not harming thirty thousand of its artisans and engineers, whom they sent to the Mongol lands. By 1221, Chinghiz had conquered Central Asia and modern Afghanistan, and two of his generals Jebe and Subotei had reached all the way to the Crimea before joining the other Mongol troops. At his death in August of 1227 Chinghiz was campaigning against the rebellious Tanguts in Northwest China. His body was transported to northeast Mongolia, where he was buried and forty young women and at least forty horses were sacrificed at his tomb.[35]

In between the Mongol troops had already attacked and taken Albania, Georgia and Armenia who had agreed to give the tribute known as *mal* and *t'agar* and to come out to them with their cavalry, wherever they led them. The tartars, agreeing to this, ceased their killing and destroying the country and themselves returned to their place. But they left a captain, Tara Buya (Qara Buqa) by name to demolish all of the strong holds, which had been conquered. They destroyed even to the foundations the impregnable forts built by the Arabs at a great cost.[36]

It has widely been accepted by the scholars that the Mongol conquests were not only the most far-reaching in the world history they also had the most radical consequences. At Chingiz Khan's death, the Mongol Empire embraced approximately half of the then known world, the largest contiguous land empire in the history of mankind. It controlled on expanse of territory stretching from the Pacific Ocean to the eastern shores of the Mediterranean and ruled over a multitude of peoples and states differing widely in language, cultural traditions, and forms of social and economic organization. The slaughter of people and the destruction of towns were not, however, the only features of Chingiz Khan's operations. In the area that he united under his rule, close contacts occurred between countries that had hitherto hardly known of each other's existence, on account of their geographical situation and the unsafe conditions that had formerly prevailed. The empire included two old cultural centers, China and Persia, which now associated more intensively as member states. The whole of Asia was opened up; trade in particular benefited from the new order. This was possible because after the conquests the disciplines embodied in the *Yasa* were introduced in the subjected countries. These rulers were undoubtedly harsh, but they brought about a large measure of security and peace, named the *Pax Mongolica.* Was it not amazing that the nomads gave the 'world culture' what could not be given by the 'cultures of the world' during that period.[37]

For forty years Chingiz Khan had been compacting the nomadic races, forging them into a mighty weapon, and then leading them across the vast spaces of Asia in a campaign of victory unexampled in history, trampling mighty realm under the feet of his horses and upon their ruins making the Mongols supreme power over the world. When the *Khakan* mounted the throne, his people had neither food for their stomach nor clothing for their bodies. It was wholly due to his labours and to his deeds that a poor nation had grown rich, and one which was few in numbers became strong and full of multitudes.

After the death of Chingiz, the process of Mongol expansion continued for more than half a century afterwards by his sons and grandsons. To acquire the greater part of Eurasian landmass and by overthrowing the Kin and Sung dynasties in China, liquidating the Abbasid Calphate and launching armies into South East Asia, the Punjab, Syria, Anatolia and Slav Europe, the Mongols were successful. The empire had three distinct phases. The first phase covered the career of Chingiz Khan and the creation of military machine, which made possible the subsequent conquests. The second dated from 1229 to 1259 (The reign of Uktai, Kuyuk and Mangu Khan) and was marked by further territorial expansion as well as by the consolidation of what had already been won. The third phase began in 1264 when Qubalai Khan won his brother Mangu's heritage and lasted until the fragmentation of the empire in the early fourteenth century.[38]

The unbroken success of the Mongols stood mighter as each victory, each conquest had brought new wives and new children. Every man fallen in battle had left a dozen offspring or more. Chingiz's son Juchi, his brother Kasar, had each of them forty children; one of his nephew had a hundred. During the reign of his grandson Kublai Khan, the number of their offsprings had swelled to eight hundred. Three decades after Chigiz's death, his own descendants were reckoned at ten thousand. According to Juvaini "The children and grand children of Chingiz Khan are more than ten thousand, each of whom has his own position (*maqam*), *yurt*, army and equipment. To record them all is impossible; our purpose in relating this much was to show the harmony which prevails among them as compared with what is related concerning other kings, how brother falls upon brother and son mediates the ruin of father till of necessity they are vanquished and conquered as their authority is downfallen and overthrown. . . . Where as by mutual aid and assistance those Khans of the children of Chingiz Khan that succeeded him on the throne have conquered the whole world and utterly annihilated their enemies."[39]

Moreover, it was always the most distinguished or boldest among the Mongols who acquired the largest number of women and the most beautiful, the ruling stock continued to improve. One may agree with the more recently view expressed in the *Washington Post* Chinggis Qahan Man of the Millennium, describing him as 'an apostle of extremes who embodies the half-civilized, half-savage duality of the human race'. Tongue-in cheek, the Post rejected Columbus for the millennial honour as 'something being'.[40]

Having no opponents left in the territory he governed and which he reckoned as one year's journey, Chingiz proceeded to teach his sons and relations the benefits of unity by the sort of arguments we find in Aesop's Fables.[41] They remembered his teachings for just twenty- four years after they began to kill each other with those refinements of cruelty which they had learnt from him. Chingiz's idea seems to have been that his four sons and their descendant should have their separate *uluses* and that the unity of his family and his empire should be maintained in a Qaan, nominated by his predecessor and accepted by a *quriltai* or Assembly of princes and high officers after his death. The expansion of the Mongol empire continued till Chingiz's grandson's Mangu, Hulegu and Qubalai. Thereafter its separate parts began to shrink. He had divided his empire between his four sons but civil wars and revolutions made many changes. However, there were no enemies to fear and we find the following *uluses* or kingdoms under the descendant of Chingiz.[42]

In the customary tribal fashion, Chingiz divided his empire among his four sons of his principal wife (including actually the son of his eldest son, who had died). Eventually, after his numerous grandsons had helped to expand it, the empire was composed of four main khanates: **A.** Great Khan (East Asia): Ogedoi (third son of Chingiz), has chosen his capital at Qaraqorum in Mongolia, 1229-41; Mongke (Mangu) grandson of Chingiz—1251-59; Khubilai, 1260-94 ruled over all China after 1279; Mongols were expelled from China by the Ming in 1368. **B.** Khanate of Chaghatai: Chaghatai (second son of Chingiz) 1227-42; **C.** Khanate of Persia (Il-Khans) built up by Halaku grandson of Chingiz after the capture of Baghdad in 1258 dissolution after 1335. **D.** Khanate of Kipchak (Golden Horde) on lower Volga: built by Batu grandson of Chingiz 1227-55, dominated Russia consquered by Tamerlane and broken up in fifteenth century.[43]

In completing their expansion over most of the known world, Mongol commanders and their mixed Mongol Turkish armies overran Persia by 1231, plundered Mesopotamia, took over Armenia and Georgia and subsequently extinguished the Abbasid Caliphate at Baghdad in 1258. In the same period, when other forces in East Asia were completing the conquest of the rest of North China (by 1241) and Korea (finally conquered in 1258), the West Asian armies erupted westward toward Europe. Under Batu they crossed the Volga (1237), burned Moscow, seized Kiev, and invaded Poland, Bohemia, Hungary and the Danube Valley (1241). At the western end of the great Eurasian steppe, they reached the Dalmatian coast of the Adriatic Sea. Poised for the invasion of Western Europe. Batu received news of the "Great Khan" Ogedei's death in 1241 in Mongolia and withdrew his whole army to South Russia so as to participate in the choice of a successor. Thus, the Western Christendom, disunited or unprepared, was saved by Mongol domestic politics.[44]

Batu's successors of the so-called Golden Horde ruled for two hundred years in South Russia, and thus two giant countries of Russia and China have a certain degree of common background, both having felt the heavy hand of Mongol despotism. Meanwhile, the so-called Ilkhans (meaning vassal khans who were subordinate to the Great Khan) ruled for a century in Persia. Both these western Khanates formed centers of power far from the Great Khan's rule in China.[45] Besides these the third most important was the khanate of Chaghatai which was surrounded by all his co-brothers and remained a great center of power and politics during Chigiz's numerous descendants throughout the period. And it always demanded much attention from the Great Khan. It was the Chaghatais who sent their expedition into the far distant places of Hindustan. It is the same region where we find Timur rising in power making Samarkand as his capital.

Bibliography

1. Bat-Ochir Bold, *Mongolian Nomadic Society: A Reconstruction of the 'Medieval' History of Mongolia* (Survey, 2001), p. 2.
2. *Comparative History of Civilizations in Asia,* Volume I, op.cit., p. 363 and Marshall G.S. Hodgson, *The Venture of Islam,* volume two [Lahore, 2004], pp. 286-92, 371-373, 386-387 and 396-404. The word Mongol is derived from the word Mong meaning brave, daring, bold. See Pringle Kennedy, *History of the Great Moghuls* (Calcutta 1933), p. 11.
3. *History of the World Conqueror,* pp. 20-21.
4. *Tabakat-I-Nasiri,* p. 936
5. Sechin Jagchid and Paul Hyer, *Mongolia's Culture and Society* (1979), p. 9.
6. *Khubilai Khan,* p. 3 and also "Some notes on the Horse Policy of the Yuan Dynasty" by Jagchid and L R Bawden in *Central Asiatic Journal* 10:3-4 (December 1965), pp. 246-68.
7. Tatars, a war-loving people, lived to the north of China, and since eighth century they had conducted plundering expeditions across the border. The Chinese considered them the most important tribe in that region and recognition of this fact led all tribes living in present day Mongolia to be labelled 'Tatars'. As a result the world empire of the Mongols is sometimes known as the Tatar empire, even after Chingiz Khan had virtually rooted out the tribe. The name Tatars was brought back to the west by Europeans travelling to the Far East in the

thirteenth and fourteenth centuries; so it also came into use in Europe, though there the atltered form 'Tartars' is often used,. See Hartog, *Russia and the Mongol Yoke,* p. 19. Today all these tribe would be collectively designated Mongols. See Gavin Hambly and others *Central Asia,* (London 1968), pp. 86-87.

8. Stanley Lane—Poole, *The Mohammadan Dynbasties,* Republished (New York, 1965], pp. 201-2.
9. Gavin Hambly, op.cit., p. 87.
10. Edwin O. Reischauer and John K. Fairbank, *East Asia: The Great Tradition* (Bostons, 1960), p. 261.
11. *Tabakat-I-Nasiri, p. 935.* Compare with a legend in an Arminian text about the origin of Chingiz Khan and his *Yasa.* It tells that "when the chief of all tribes and nation was called on Busx and of these nations one was called Tuyark which were called Tatars, this race went from Turkestan, their own country, and moved to a region somewhere in the east. They abode as robbers and savages and were very poor for a long time. They had no kind of religion save idols of felt, needed for sorcery, which they always carried with them, but they paid reverence to the sun, as a manifestation of divine power. When they unexpectedly came to realize their position, being much oppressed by their poor miserable and poor life, they invoked the aid of God, the creater of heaven and earth, and they made a great covenant with him to abide by his commands. An angel appeared to them by the command of God in the guise of an eagle with golden feathers, and spoke in their own speech and tongue to their chief, who was named Cankez The latter went and stood before the angel in the guise of an eagle at a distance—the length of a bow shot. Then the eagle told them all the commandments of God. These are the precepts of God which he imposed on them, and which they themselves called yasax."

    "The first is this: that ye love one another; second do not commit adultery; do not steal; do not bear false witness; do not betray anyone. Respect the aged and poor. If a transgressor of such be found among them, the law breakers are to be put to death." When the angel had imparted this, he named their chief Tayan, whom they called Cankez Tayan or Cankez Xan. The angel bade them rule over many countries and districts and to multiply without limit and in countless numbers, which also came to pass. See *History of the Nation of the Archers* (Cambridge, 1954], pp. 21-23.
12. *The Journey of William of Rubruck,* Introduction, pp. xvi-xvii.
13. *East Asia: The Great Tradition,* op.cit, p. 261.
14. Ibid., p. 263.
15. *Secret History of the Mongols,* pp. 13-16. For his boyhood and youth see pp.17-34. For swearing oath of loyalty and making Temujin as Khan and also assigning duties to them by Chingiz see, pp. 49-52 and p. 133.

16. *Tabakat-i-Nasiri,* pp. 942-53.
17. *East Asia: The Great Tradition,* pp. 263-64.
18. Mirja Juntunen & Birgit N. Schlyter (Ed.], *Return to the Silk Routes: Current Scandinavian Research on Central Asia (London, 1999], pp. 75-76.* The name of famous conqueror has been spelled in many different ways—e.g. Genghiz, Gengis, Zingis, Tchinguiz etc. See. *Heart of Asia,* p. 149n.1.
19. *Secret History of the Mongols,* pp. 133-58.
20. *Tabakat-i-Nasiri,* p. 953.
21. *East Asia: The Great Tradition,* p. 264.
22. *History of the World Conqueror,* pp. 23-24.
23. *Tabakat-i-Nasiri,* p. 954.
24. Ibid., pp. 960-62.
25. *History of Mankind,* p. 218.
26. *East Asia: The great Tradition,* p. 265.
27. *The Journey of William of Rubruck, Introduction,* pp. xiv-xvi. Vladimirtsov devotes a full chapter on "Chingiz-Khan in daily life" in his book *The Life of Chingis Khan.* In this Chapter he gives a quote which is worth mentioning for Chingiz's idea about a true Mongol. He says: 'In everyday life behave like a two-year-old calves, but in battle be like hawks; at feasts and entertainments be like young colts, but in battle fly at the enemy like falcons; in broad daylight be alert like any old wolf and in the night's darkness cautious like the black ravena," p. 161.
28. Ibid., p. 4.
29. *Secret History of the Mongols,* pp. 126-28.
30. *East Asia: The Great Tradition,* p. 266.
31. *Khubilai Khan,* p. 6. It has been suggested that Chingiz used three types of ties called *quda, anda and nokor* which he used with enormous skill and foresight as the means to unite a sprawling and shifting population and create a superb fighting machine. For details see *Secret History of the Mongols,* pp. 7-8.
32. *C/F Jamial-tawarikh* (ed. B. Karimi), Tehran, 1959, vol. II, p. 688 in 'The Yuan Dynasty and the Uighurs of Turfan' in M. Rossabi (ed.), *China Among Equals,* p. 244.
33. Ibid., pp. 244-45.
34. Gavin Hambly, op.cit., p. 99 and *The Venture of Islam,* pp. 288-92.
35. *Khublai Khan,* pp. 6-7 There were many factors that provided the success to Chingiz's conquests. It is natural the newly revived feudal and military state of the Mongols had great advantages over the old empires and kingdoms which existed then In most territories of Central Asia and which in their majority had degraded by their internal contradictions and animosity. No less role had been played by Chingiz himself as a great politician and a military genius of his time. The light cavalary equipped with tough swift-footed Mongol horses and bows

always was the main force of Chingiz Khan. But his military skills consisted in the fact that he had made a great innovation in the art of war by having taken over new techniques and improving them with the help of Chinese and Mongol experts. He had even gun powder canon used in sapping operations during his western campaign. See Sh. Bira, "The Mongol Empire And Its East and West Relations" in R.C Sharma, K. Warikov, M. Haider and Sh. Bira[Ed], *Mongolia: Culture, Economy and Politics* (Indian-Mongolian Assessment), (New Delhi 1992), p. 74. Also see *History of the Nation of the Archers*, pp. 291-93 and *Secret History of the Mongols*, p. 18.

36. *History of the Nation of the Archers*, pp. 293-97. Also p. 386n.22 in which meanings of *mal* have given as herds, property. In Mongolian and Turkish it means cattle and the meaning of t'agar as "provisions for horses", a tax on grains and foodstuffs.
37. Leo De Hartog, *Genghis Khan* op.cit p. 144 and Thomas T. Allsen. 'The Yuan Dynasty and the Uigheers of Turfan in the 13th Century' in M. Rossabi (ed.) *China Among Equals* (Berkeley, 1983), p. 243.
38. Gavin Hambly, *Central Asia*, op.cit., p. 100.
39. *History of the World Conqueror*, p. 43.
40. Quoted from *Washington Post* December 31, 1995 See, *Secret History*, Introduction, p. 5.
41. Juvaini writes that one day Chingiz Khan called his sons together and taking an arrow from his quiver he broke it in half. Then he took two arrows and broke them also. And he continued to add to the bundle until there were so many arrows that even athletes were unable to break them. Then turning to his sons he said: 'So it is with you also. . . .' See *History of the World Conqueror*, p. 41.
42. *Compressive History of India*, volume V, p. 84.
43. *East Asia: Great Tradition*, pp. 267-70. See also *History of the World Conqueror*, pp. 42-43.
44. East Asia: Great Tradition, p. 270.
45. Ibid., p. 270.

3

The Chaghatai Khanate

THE ONLY TRULY Central Asian and nomadic vision of the Mongol empire was the appanage of Chinghiz Khan's second son, Chaghatai. Named after its ruler, the Chaghatai Khanate though covered Turkestan and Transoxania, it never possessed precise borders. The sources on the boundaries of the Chaghatais are not unanimous. *The Secret History of the Mongols* speaks on the issue but very vaguely. On the occasion of Chingiz Khan's declaring Ogodei as his successor he spoke to his sons Juchi and Chaghatai, declared, "Mother Earth is wide: its rivers and waters are many. Extending the camps (the grazing grounds) that can easily be divided, we shall make each of you rule over a domain and we shall separate you." And he said, "you Joci and Ca'adai, keep to your words:

Do not let yourselves be scorned by people,
Do not let yourselves be laughed at by men.[1]

Juvaini states that when the lands of Transoxiana and Turkestan were subjugated, his camping grounds and those of his children and armies extended from Besh-Baligh to Samarqand, fair and pleasant places fit to be the abode of kings. In spring and summer he had his quarters in Almaligh and Quyas.[2] Rashid al Din places the lands and *yurts* from Altai, which was the *yurt* of the Naiman people to the banks of the Oxus under Chaghatai.[3]

In the introduction of *Tarikh-i-Rashidi*, we find that Mawarnnahr or Transoxiana was the central kingdom of Chaghatai situated chiefly between the rivers Syr and Amu but included in its extension towards the north-east, the hill ranges and steppes lying beyond the right bank of the Syr, east of the Kipchak plains, and west of lakes Issigh-kul and Ala-Nor. Towards the east, the Chaghatai domain took in the greater part of the region now known as Chinese (or Eastern) Turkistan, Farghana (or Khokand) and Badakshan; while towards the south it embraced Kunduz, Balkh, and, at the outset, Khurasan—a country which, at that time, spread eastward to beyond Herat and Ghazni, and southward to Mekran. This was, perhaps, the most extensive appanage of all, and within its limits were to be found the greatest variety of races and tribes, and the greatest diversity of modes of life. It comprised, on the one hand, some of the richest in Asiatic civilization, and some of the most flourishing cities in Asia; while, on the other hand, source of the rudest hill tribes or Hazaras as they were called then, had their homes in the southern highlands, and large tracts of barren steppe-land were occupied by almost equally primitive nomads, who drove their flocks from hill to valley and valley to hill, in search of pasture, according to season.[4]

More or less Lane-Poole supports the same view and states that Chaghatai was allotted the appanage of Ma-wara-l-nahr, or Transoxiana (Bukharia), with part of Kashghar, Badakhshan, Balkh and Ghazna, and who founded the Khanate of those region.[5] In another study we find that hostile both to the supreme Khan in China and to other Mongol dynasties that accepted his overlordship, was the Chaghatay Mongol power in Syr and Oxus basins, the Yedisu steppes northeast thereof, and the Kabul mountains, which also came to control the Punjab.[6]

Yule in his *Cathay and the way thither* suggests that, the tract assigned by Chingiz, in the distribution of his provinces, to his son Chaghatai; embraced Mawarannahr (or Transoxiana) and part of Khwarizm, the Uighur country, Kashghar, Badakshan, Balkh, and the province of Ghazni to the banks of the Sindh; or in modern geography, the kingdoms of Independent Tartary with the exception of Khiva or the greater part of it, the country under the Uzbeks of Kunduz, Afghanistan, and the western and northern portions of Chinese Turkestan, including Dzungaria. Besh-Baligh, north of the Tien Shan, was at first the headquarters of the *Khans*, but it was afterwsards transforred to Almaliq.[7]

According to Bertold Spular, the region between the Amu Darya (Oxus) and Mongolia, inhabited for centuries by Turkic peoples for the most part, had already been part of the Mongol empire during the lifetime of Chingiz Khan. Before Persia had been properly brought under control—that is to say, during the first fifty years of the Empire's history—this had been the southern border of the Empire, and in consequence had formed the assembly point of its armies before embarking on new campaigns. It had been administered in an unusual manner: Chinghiz Khan had allotted it to his son, Chaghatai, but he had not defined the frontier between this part of the Empire and the kingdom of Ogodai. As the two brothers acted independently in the region, there were occasional clashes.[8] Barthold too speaks about Chaghatai's *yurt* stretched from Uyghuria to Samarqand and Bukhara and from the southern Altai to the Amu Darya.[9]

The Mongol dynasty in China ruled barely a hundred years, but within that time the Mongols, who had followed their rulers in their Eastern conquests had given up the heathenism of their native land and had become Buddhists. In Western Persia and in the countries round about Persia, the Mongols had become Muslims and were living under conditions far different from those that rule in their native steppes whence

Chingiz Khan had called them forth to conquer. But those of the race who had remained in Central Asia were for hundreds of years much what they had been before, true Nomads, pasturing enormous flocks, despising agriculture and crowded towns. The division of the Central Khanate whose first ruler was Chaghatai, a son of Chingiz, into Western and Eastern Khanates, in the beginning of the fourteenth century, the Western being constituted of Mawarannahr with its numerous towns and its far spread agriculture and the Eastern being the North-Western part of the country now known as Chinese Turkestan, cut off the Mongols of the west.

In other words in Persia and China, the Mongol rulers, who linked their destines with those of their sedentary subjects, inevitably began to lose their Mongol identity. But in the Central Asian heartland, the descendants of Chaghatai and Ogodei, sons of Chingiz, maintained traditional steppe politics geared to the interests of their nomad followers and increasingly opposed to the policies of the great Khan in China and his ally, the Ilkhan, in Persia.[10]

In the *Secret History of the Mongol,* Chingiz Khan said, "Ca'adai is headstrong and is, by nature, punctilious. Koke Cos (the adviser) shall stay at his side evening and morning, and shall tell him his thinks (he shall advise him)."[11] It is mentioned that when Chaghatai was born—the starry sky was turning upon itself. The many people were in turmoil. They did not enter their beds to rest. But fought against each other, the crusty earth was turning and turning. The entire nation was in turmoil: They (people) did not enter their coverlets to rest, but attacked each other. On the occasion of Chingiz Khan's declaring his successor, Chaghatai had a quarrel with his brother Juchi. Both stood holding each other by the collar. After a detailed conversation and advised by his Koko Cos ultimately the matter was resolved.[12]

About his earlier carrier we find Chaghatai accompanying his brothers Juchi and Ogodei during a campaign towards Khwarizm and setting their camp at Urganj which was captured later on.[13]

When Ogedai was declared as *qan*, Chaghatai, the elder brother installed him on the throne. The night-guards, the quiver-bearers and the eight thousand day-guards who had been protecting the previous life of their father Chinghiz Khan, the personal slaves and the ten thousand guards who had been in close attendance on the person of his father, the *qan*, were all handed over by elder brother Chaghatai and Tuli to Ogodei Qan. The domains of the center they handed over to him in the same manner. Ogodei after consulting Chaghatai sent a troop under Oqotur and Monggetv in the west for further annexing those territories.[14]

In *Jamiut Tawarikh* also we find the same account where we are informed that Chaghatai spared no efforts to seat Uktae upon the throne of the Khanate and went to great pains to him so enthroned in accordance with his father's command. Together with Tuli and the other kinsmen, he knelt nine times and made obeisance. And although he was the elder brother he used to treat Uktae with the utmost respect and rigidly observe the niceties of etiquette. The author gives an example and writes that one day they were riding on easy-paced horses and Chaghatai being drunk, said to Uktae: "Let us race our horses for a bet." And having made a bet, they ran a race, and Chaghatai's horse, being a little faster, won by a head. At night in his tent, Chaghatai was reminded of this incident and he reflected: "How was it possible for me to make a bet with Qa'an and let my horse beat his? Such conduct was a great breach of etiquette. Judging by this we and others are becoming insolent, and this will lead to harm." And before morning he summoned the emirs and said: "Yesterday I was guilty of a crime of committing such an action. Let us go to Uktae so that he may convict me of my crime and carry whatever is a fitting punishment." And setting out with the emirs in a great throng he came to the audience hall earlier than usual. The guards reported to Uktae that Chaghatai had come with a great multitude, and Uktae, although he had complete confidence in him, was apprehensive of the situation, wondering what his motive could be. He sent some persons to his brother to ask him. (Chaghatai) said: "we, all of us, *aqa* and *ini,* spoke great words in the *qurittai* and gave written undertakings that Uktae was the Qa'an and we should tread the path of loyalty and obedience and in no way oppose him. Yesterday, I made a bet and raced my horse against his. What right have we to make a bet with the Qa'an. Therefore, I am guilty and have come to confess my guilt and submit to punishment. Whether he puts me to death or beats me is for him to decide." Uktae Qa'an was filled with shame at these words. He became more loving and tender and humbled himself before his brother, but though he sent someone to say, "what words are these? He is my *aqa.* Why pay attention to such trifles?" (Chaghatai) would not listen. However, in the end, he agreed that the Qa'an should spare his life and made an offering of nine horses. The *bitikchis* proclaimed that the *Qa'an* had spared Chaghatai's life, so that everyone heard and knew that he was making the offering because he had been pardoned. He then entered the *ordo* and explained this to all present with the eloquence that he possessed. On this account the concord between them increased, the Qa'an made his son Guyuk his attendant and placed him in his guard, where he used to serve him. And Chaghatai's greatness became such as cannot be described . . . in all important affairs Qa'an used to consult Chaghatai and would undertake nothing without his adriceand approval.[15]

Chaghatai was always treated in high esteem and was consulted in matters of policy. It was he who set an example to send the eldest son on the campaigns which was followed by Ogodei. According to Chaghatai, "If the eldest of the sons goes into the field, the army will be larger than before. . . ." Such was the way in which he sent Batu, Buri, Guyuk, Mongke and the other princes into the field.[16]

On an occasion when there was a conflict among the

princes, Chaghatai was given a hand to decide the matter.[17] Credit of setting up post-station connecting the all kingdoms with each other goes to Chaghatai and many more measures were taken with his approval.[18] In the account of Chang Chun we find that when Chaghatai was following his father to the west (in 1219), first made a way through the mountain covered to their summit with dense forests, cut through the rocks, and built forty eight bridges with the wood cut on the mountains. The bridges were so wide that two carts could pass side by side.[19]

Chaghatai was a fierce and mighty Khan, stern and severe. When the land of Transoxiana and Turkestan were subjugated, his camping ground and those of his children and armies extended from Besh-Baligh to Samarqand, fair and pleasant places fit to be the abode of kings. In spring and summer he had his quarters in Almaligh and Quyas, which in those seasons resembled the Garden of Iram. He constructed large pools, which were called *kol*, a Turkish world for lake in the region for the flocking of the waterfowl. He also built a town called Qutlugh. The autumn and winter he spent in (Marauzik?), on the Ila. And at every stage, from beginning end he had laid up stores of food and drink. And he was ever engaged in amusements and pleasures and dallying with sweet-faced peri-like maidens.

He was the custodian of *Yasa* and for fear of his *Yasa* and punishment his followers were so well disciplined that during his reign no traveller, so long as he was near his army, had need of guard or patrol on any stretch of the road and as is said by way of hyperbole, a woman with a golden vessel on her head might walk alone without fear or dread. And he enacted minute *yasas* that were an intolerable imposition upon such as the Taziks, e.g. that none might slaughter meat in the Moslem fashion nor sit by day in running water, and so on. The *yasa* forbidding the slaughter of sheep in lawful manner he sent to every land; and for a time no man slaughtered sheep openly in Khurasan and Moslems were forced to eat carrion. When Chingiz Khan died Chaghatai's court became the rendezvous of all mankind and men journeyed from near and far to do him homage. But it was not long before a sore disease attacked him such that the "cause was victor over the cure". Habash Ahmad, who had been attached to Chaghatai's service ever since the conquest of Transoxiana and had attained to the rank of *Vizir*, still remained in the service of Chaghatai's widow.[20]

The *yasa* had been dictated by Chingiz Khan from time to time, and traced on leaves of gold by his secretaries. These leaves of the Law were only to be touched by the children of his house, who brought them forth at the councils. They were the Bible and the code of the nomads, immutable as fate according to Harold Lamb. He further states: "If the descendants born after me." Chingiz had said, "keep to the *Yasa* and do not change it; for a thousand and ten thousand years the Everlasting Sky will aid and preserve them." Neither Ogedai, nor his brothers could read the tracings on the gold leaves. But they had careful memory of the illiterate for the spoken word, and they knew every saying the *yasa*—or, at least, Chaghatai did. The Wild Horse (Chaghatai) had the duty of enforcing the law.[21]

Chaghati—the Wild Horse—was, as his father had been, a nomad to the core. Cautious, sparing of words, he cherished tribal customs. He drank alone, and he punished savagely. He craved new women, but as with Tului—no woman could influence him. A sorcerer kept at his side, feeding his superstition with magical tricks. Although the Wild Horse brooded over the supernatural, men dreaded his anger. He was unyielding as the stone of his mountain gorges. In his dominion no guards kept the roads or the city gates. It was said that a virgin could go unattended, carrying a jar of gold pieces in safety from one end of his lands to the other.[22] Chaghatai could enforce the law against himself without mercy, which has already been mentioned how he asked the Qa'an to punish him on the matter of a bet between the two. He took active part in the investment of Otrar[23] and was dispatched with his brother Ogetai against Khwarizm which was deserted at that time by the Sultan leaving behind certain chiefs and successfully infested it and made the town, the abode of the jackal and the haunt of owl and kite; pleasure was far removed from its houses and its castles were reduced to desolation.[24] Later he was asked to pursue Jalaluddin Mangbarni from Kirman.[25]

After completing the mission Chaghatai and Ogedei went to a place called Qara-Kol (literary Black Lake in Uzbekistan) where they were allowed to enjoy their stay with hunting of the swan and every week, as a sample of their hunting, they would send Chingiz Khan fifty camel-loads of swans.[26] When Chingiz Khan died Chaghatai was in Quyas (in the neighbourhood of Almaligh) from where he came to attend the *quriltai.* Chaghatai was the main figure in establishing Ogedei on the throne,[27] and joined him in the campaign against Khitai region.[28]

The Chaghatais had no conception of how to establish a regular state on western pattern or on that of Chinese or Persia. For this they lacked the historical background. Their cousins of Kubalai's house or of the house of Hulegu in Persia, had found at their disposal the age old tradition of ancient centralized empires—whole history of administrative customs of *yamens* and divans. They became the sons of Heaven here, sultans there. They could identify themselves with states that were sharply defined, geographically and historically as well as culturally. Jagatai's son had nothing like this. Their realm with its shifting boundaries had as its center no Peking or Tabriz but prairie. It never occurred to them to settle in Kashghar or Khotan, in the Tarim oasis, for there were gardens enclosed, too small for their herds and cavalry.

The fate of this Central Asiatic region was determined by its situation. Being no more than the weak centre of powerful bordering territories, confined in all directions by the great Mongolian "local khanates" of the Yuan Emperors, the Ilkhans and the Golden Horde, it had no possibility of expansion. Every attempt of the restless nomad masses to pass beyond the circumscribed frontier resulted in overwhelming defeat. Since the nomads were thus deprived of the possibility of expansion, their surplus energies found went in unceasing fratricidal war, so that for the next half century the realm of Chaghatai knew no rest.[29] However, later they ventilated their energy towards India.

It is reflection on the nomadic traditions of life retained by the Chaghatai Khan for longer than China, Persia or Kipchak. So long as they controlled the steppes north of the Tien Shan, which provided them with excellent grazing grounds and a regular supply of horses and warriors they took little interest in oases of Mawarannahr and Kashgharia except as source of revenue. Wassaf records how Barqa Khan (1264-70) even plundered his own cities of Samarqand and Bukhara before crossing the Amu Darya to raid Ilkhanid Khurasan. This is how much of the region had suffered greatly during the foundation of the Mongol empire.[30] Ibn Battuta visiting Mawarannahr a hundred year later, was appalled by the decay of urban life. Tirmiz, for example, had been rebuilt upon a new site following its sack by Chingiz Khan, but Samarqand still contained extensive ruins, while in Khurasan, Merv was still uninhabited and Balkh absolutely desolate.[31]

Chaghatai died 7 months before Uktae Khan, in the year 638/1241-42. Ogedei Khan died on 11 December 1241.[32] According to Juvaini, Chaghatai had many sons and grandsons, but his eldest son Metiken, having been killed at Bamiyan and Qara Hulegu having born at that time, Chingiz Khan, and after him Qa'an and Chaghatai, had made him Chaghatai's heir successor. In accordance with this ruling, after Chaghatai's death, his wife Yesulun, Habash Amid-al-Mulk and the Pillars of the state favoured his claim. But when Guyuk Khan was made Qa'an, having a friendship for Yesu-Mongke, who was Chaghatai's own son, he said: 'why should the grandson succeed when there is a son?' Accordingly he set up Yesu in his father's kingdom and entrusted him with the direction of affairs of state.[33]

Rashiduddin states that although Qara-Hulegu was the most senior of Chaghatai's descendants and the eldest son of Mo'etuken, nevertheless Guyuk Khan sent him instead to rule over the *ulas* of Chaghatai, because Yesu-Mongke, the fifth son of Chaghatai, was opposed to Mongke Qa'an.

Now according to Juvaini, Yesu was constantly carousing; he was ignorant of sobriety and made intoxication a habit, drinking wine from morning till evening. When he came firmly established in the kingdom he grew angry with Habash Amid because of his having supported Qara-Hulegu; and he plotted against him. Habash was replaced by one Baha-ad-Din who performed all the ceremonies and courtesies of respect and several times restrained Yesu from carrying out the designs he had upon Habash 'Amid. Yesu continued to reign until Mengu Qa'an son of Tuli son of Chinghiz ascended the throne of the Khanate. Yesu opposed his accession, whereupon Mengu Qa'an settled the kingdom upon Qara Helagu by virtue of the earlier testament. He distinguished Qara with all kinds of favours and sent him home. Upon the way back according to Juvaini, the inevitable hour prevented him from reaching his *ordu.*[35] Rashiduddin also informs that when Mengu Qa'an became Qa'an, he gave Qara Hulegu a *yarligh* commanding him to put Yesu Mongke to death and as heir-apparent, become the ruler of that *ulus.* Qara Hulegu died *enroute* before reaching the *ulus.*[36]

Mengu Qa'an settled the kingdom upon his son; and since the latter was as yet but a child, he placed the keys of government in the hands of Orqina, Qara's widow. When she returned to her *ordu,* Yesu also by Batu's leave, shortly afterwards arrived home. To him also Fate gave no quarter.[37] Rashiduddin explains that Orqina Khatun put Yesu Mongke to death in accordance with the *yarligh* and ruled herself in her husband's stead.[38] In the end Juvaini tells how Emir

Habash and his son returned to power and they managed to get rid of Bahauddin.[39]

For further history of the Chaghatais we have to depend upon Rashiduddin. When Mongke Qa'an passed away, his successor Qubilai Qa'an sent Abishaqa, who was the eldest son of Buri, the second son of Moetuken, to marry Orqina Khatun and rule the *ulus* of Chaghatai in place of Qara Hulegu. Here Rashidudin confuses, as we know Qara Hulegu had already died. He also does not mention Abishqa's name in the table IV pertaining to the Chaghatai Khanate.[40] However, in the account of the Buri second son of Moetuken, he mentions Abishqa as the first son of Buri. At the time of Ariq Boke's revolt against Qubilai, he was in the service of the Qa'an. He was sent to take the place of Qara Hulegu as ruler of the *ulus* of Chaghatai and marry Orqina Khatun. On the way he was taken prisoner by Ariq Boke's troops and remained with them until Asutai, the son of Mongke Khan, who was allied with Ariq Boke, put him to death.[41] At another place Rashiduddin states that when Qubilai Qa'an sent messengers to Ariq Boke for submission. They dispatched Abishqa with his younger brother Nariu-Qadan, the son of Buri, the son of Moetuken, over his grandfather's *ulus.* On the border of the Tangqut (Tangut of Juvaini) country they were met by the envoys of Ariq Boke with a large force of men, who seized them and brought them before him. They were imprisoned and kept in custody.[42]

On the stage of Central Asia, this time appears Alghu son of Baidar, the sixth son of Chaghatai, who played an important role and ultimately became the ruler of the *ulus* (1260-1265/6]. Mongke Qa'an's death in August 1259 led to a struggle for the throne between two of his brothers, Qubilai and Ariq Boke and in 1260 two rival *quriltais* enthroned both brothers as rival Qa'ans.[43] Rashiduddain mentions that Alghu, the son of Baider, the sixth son of Chaghatai became the ruler of the *ulus* of Chaghatai by command of Ariq Boke and married Orqina Khatun.[44] At another place he writes that Ariq Boke gave him a *yarligh* appointing ruler of the *ulus* and commanding him to guard those frontiers against the army of Qubilai Khan and that of Chaghatai's descendants and to collect money, provisions, and equipment for the army from the provinces of Turkistan and to send it all to him so that he might proceed with an easy mind to make war on the army of Qubilai Qa'an. Alghu arrived and communicated the *yarligh,* and established himself as ruler. Here our author differs from his earlier statement that Alghu married Orqina Khatun. He states that Orqina Khatun went to Ariq Boke and made complaints about Alghu. She remained there for a while, and after some time Ariq Boke sent envoys to those parts to levy two out of every ten cattle and to arrange (the supply of) great quantities of money and arms for the army. Rashiduddin gives the names of envoys—Erkegun, Buritei Bitikchi, and Shadi. They set off and, having delivered the *yarligh* to Alghu, began to collect the cattle, money, and arms in that province. When a certain amount had been assembled, they sent it off. In 661/1262-63 Alghu detained them on the plea that other *nokers* were still there, hence all should have left together. Then, there was an argument on this issue and Alghu seized and imprisoned them and broke his relations with Ariq Boke in favour of Qubilai Khan. Accordingly he put the ambassadors to death and retained all those goods and arms. Alghu's position was greatly strengthen thereby, and Orqina Khatun having returned, he married her and secured absolute possession of the throne of the *ulus* of Chaghatai. When the news of these events reached Ariq Boke, he led an army against Alghu and they joined battle. In the first two encountered Ariq Boke was defeated but in the third Alghu was put to flight and came to Bukhara and Smarqand, where he seized money, arms, and animals from the rich. Ariq Boke plundered his heavy baggage and after the lapse of a year returned from that region to repel the army of Qubilai Qa'an.[45]

In the account of Qubilai Qa'an's battles with Ariq Boke for the throne we find how Alghu was involved in this struggle for power. And it seems that out of necessity and compulsion that he was sent to the *ulus* of Chaghatai. It is mentioned that there was a custom to bring food and drink for Qaraqorum on wagons from Khitai. Qubilai Qa'an banned this traffic and there occurred a great dearth and famine in that region. Ariq Boke was at his wit's end and said "the best thing is for Alghu, the son of Baidar, the son of Chaghatai, who has long been in attendance on the throne and has learnt the way and *yosum* of every matter, to go and administer his grandfather's residence and *ulus* and so send us assistance and provisions and arms and guards the frontier along the Oxus so that the army of Hulegu and the army of Berke cannot come to the aid of Qubilai Qa'an from that direction." With this idea in mind, he spoke kindly to him and sent him on his way. Alghu leapt forth like an arrow from a bow and took his own head. When he reached Kashghar nearly 150,000 mounted warriors were gathered around him, and he rose in revolt and insurrection.[46]

In the meantime we learn that Ariq Boke had sought pardon and showed loyalty toward Qubilai and promised to present himself before him till Alghu, Hulegu and Berke reached. By that time Alghu had gone to Qubilai's side and was in touch with him through his messengers. It is during this struggle that we find Qaidu, a grandson of Ogedei supporting Ariq Boke. The situation was going out of control and Qubilai made an appeal to Hulegu and Alghu, saying: "The lands are in revolt. From the banks of the Oxus to the gates of Egypt the Tazik land must be administered and well guarded by thee, Hulegu; from the Altai on the far side to the Oxus *el* and *ulus* must be administered and maintained by Alghu; and from the Altai on this side to the shores of the Ocean-Sea[all lands) will be maintained by me." But Ariq Boke did not keep his word and broke his promise and again went to war against Qubilai Qa'an. He, having several times asked Alghu to help him with arms and provisions and having received no response, he equipped an army and set out against him. Rashiduddin puts a question mark on the relations between Alghu and Ariq Boke and ends with remarks *"And God knows best what is right"*. In his next subtitle "The Revolt of Alghu against Ariq Boke and the reason thereof; he tells how he fought the army of Ariq Boke (and) was defeated; how he recovered his strength; and (how) Ariq Boke's cause began to weaken.[47]

Rashiduddin repeats what he has earlier written regarding Alghu's revolt against Ariq Boke and gives detail of the wars between the two. Alghu was successful in giving his position and marrying Orqina Khatun and to manage his *ulus* with the help of Masud Beg who was made the *sahib diwan* of his realm and sent him to Samarqand and Bukhara to administer those places. He proceeded thither and began to collect taxes continuously from the population, and dispatched them to Alghu as they came in. As a result, the affairs of Alghu recovered. He gathered his scattered forces together, fought a battle with Berke's (Khan of the Golden Horde) army, and defeated them and plundered Otrar. A year later he died and Orqina Khatun, in agreement with the emires and vizirs, set her son Mubarak Shah in his place.[48]

When Mubarak Shah became the ruler, Baraq the grandson of Moetuken, the second son of Chaghatai was in the service of Qubilai Khan, who wished that he and Mubarak Shah should jointly administer the *ulus*.[49] Baraq managed to oust Mubarak Shah convicting of some crime and made him the supervisor of his cheetah keepers. When Baraq entered Khurasan to make war on Abaqa Khan, Mubarak Shah accompanied him (at which time) he fled to Abaqa Khan.[50]

Elsewhere it has been mentioned that after the death of Alghu, the army continued as before to pillage and irregularities; but Mubarak Shah, being a Muslim, would not allow any violence against the peasants. When Ariq Boke was forced to surrender to Qubilai Khan and rebellion subdued in the region, Baraq, who had been in the attendance of the Qa'an, was sent by him to the *ulus* of Chaghatai and given a *yarligh* to the effect that Mubarak Shah and he were to rule the *ulus* (jointly). When Baraq arrived and found Mubarak Shah and Orqina firmly established and in a strong position, he did not show the *yarligh.* Mubarak Shah asked him why he had come. He replied: "For sometime I have been far away from my *ulus* and home, and my people are scattered and distressed. I have sought permission and come to gather my followers together and wander about with you." Mubarak Shah was pleased with these words, and Baraq lived with him practicing craft and dissimulation whilst gathering military men around him out of every corner. All of a sudden an emir, called Bitikchi, and certain army leaders joined him. They deposed Mubarak Shah, and Baraq became absolute ruler, while Mubarak Shah was reduced to the position of being his head cheetah-keeper.[51]

We are further informed that since the frontier of the *ulus* of Chaghatai adjoined Qaidu's territory but certain areas were occupied by Qaidu and Baraq fought several battles with him. In the first Qaidu was victorious and when they resumed hostilities with Qipchaq, the son of Qadagan, of the family Ogedei Khan, made peace between then, and they swore an oath and became *anda* (sworn brothers) to each other and to this day their descendants are also *anda* to one another.[52]

Qaidu played an important role in state building in Central Asia. He was a grandson of the Mongol Khan Ogedei who died in the year AD 1241. On the basis of *Jamiut Tawarikh,* Wassaf and Kashani it had been suggested that Qaidu, the son of Kashi, the fifth son of the Great Khan Ogedei, was born in 633/1235-36.[53] According to the report of Jamal Qarshi written in the first years of the fourteenth century, Ogedei gave blessings to Qaidu, the son of Qashi, saying, "Would that my young son will succeed me,"[54] Qaidu took part in the battles of the Mongols in Europe[55] and led one of the three main groups of the Mongol army. He received favours from Mangu Khan as the hero of the Polish and Silesian campaigns.[56] In a recent study Qaidu has been placed as one of the great Mongol Khans, and is better known as a rebel than as a state builder. He became an active player in the Mongol arena after the house of Ogodei lost its supremacy to Toluids, descendants of Chingiz's younger son.[57]

E. Bretschneider while explaining a Mongol Chinese medieval map of Central and Western Asia suggests in his introductory notices on the basis of Yule's *Cathay*, that at an early date, however, in the history of Chaghatai's dynasty, the claims of Qaidu to the supreme khanship seem to have led a partition of the Chaghatai territory, for Qaidu held under his own immediate sway a large tract, the greater part of which belonged apparently to the appendage of Chaghatai, over which Qaidu exercised superiority. It is not clear what were the limits between Qaidu's and that of the Chaghatai Khans; but it may be gathered that Qaidu's dominions included Kashghar and Yarkand, and all the cities bordering on the south side of the Tien Shan as far east as Karakhoja, as well as the valley of the Talas River, and all the country north of the Tien Shah from Lake Balkhash eastward to the Chagan Nor, and the country farther north between the upper Yenisei and the Irtysh. During a great part of Qaidu's struggles, he found a staunch ally Dua, the son of Borak, whom he had set up the throne of Chaghatai in 1272.[58]

About Qaidu, Barthold writes 'he must have been one of the most remarkable Mongol rulers'. But our information about him is scanty. His father had died of drunkenness; so he never touched any intoxicant. He was a true Mongol in appearance and had (according to Rashiduddin) only nine hair in his beard. He was with Ariq Buqa in the troubled years, 1260-64, but when Ariq decided to go and submit to Qubilai, Qaidu refrained from going with him and claimed the hereditary Qaanship of Ogedei—his grandfather. He seems to have created an army out of nothing but the courage and discipline of his army became proverbial. He did not sacrifice the interests of the civil population to the army, whose prosperity reached a high standard during his reign. Qaidu has been stated as the founder of an independent Mongol kingdom in Central Asia.[59] This idea has been further strengthened by Michal Biran in her *Qaidu and the Rise of the Independent Mongol State in Central Asia.*

To revive the cause of the Ogedei in Central Asia, by virtue of his political and military skills, from 1270s onwards Qaidu succeeded in establishing a kingdom of the house of Ogodei in Central Asia and in becoming a formidable adversary to the Great Khan—Qubilai, Mongke's brother and successor (1260-94) and his successor, Temur Oljeitu (1294-1307). Qaidu's activities undermined the Qaan's authority, shifted the balance of power in the Mongol empire and accelerated its dismemberment. Though the house of Ogodei departed from the stage of history after Qaidu's death, the Mongol state that he established in Central Asia, a state independent of the Qaan's authority survived him under the rule of the Chaghadaids, his erstwhile rivals, allies and successors.[60]

Qaidu and Buraq in joint venture began to expand their empire. Buraq invaded Khurasan but was defeated and returned and died in 1271. In 1282 Qaidu selected Dawa Khan son of Buraq to be joint ruler with him. The two khans had to fight on all fronts but they had the most prosperous region of the Mongol empire in their hands and their power expanded. Following the examples of Chingiz, Qaidu formed military divisions under the command of his sons. In the last years of his life, he entrusted to them, the defense of the marches, of the kingdom. Urus was in command of the Chinese frontier, Bey Kecher on the border of the Golden Horde and Sarban in Afghanistan from where the troops of Qaidu and Dawa gradually dislodged the forces of the Ilkhans. Dawa seems also to have followed a similar policy. The two Khans made a strong effort to expand into India, the frontier of which down to the Ravi had probably come into their hands a little before the accession of Alauddin Khalji in 1296; but the enterprise, though continued for several years, failed disastrously. Qaidu probably died in 1301 and was succeeded by his son, Chapar. Dawa survived till 1306.

The Mongols of Central Asia were too busy in fighting each other to think of foreign lands. Alauddin Tarmashirin Khan, who ascended the throne in 1326, invaded India and seemed, for a time, to carry all before him. But the invasion was a mistake for his power was too weak at home. In 1332 a revolt was led against him by one Bazan, a Muslim,on the ground that he neglected the Chingizi *yasas.* Tarmashirin tried to flee to Ghazni, but was captured and sent to Bazan, who put him to death.[61]

The other most important reason, according to an expert on frontier history, was that the Mongols of the appendage of Chaghatai, had by then become Turkish in language and Muslim in religion and had transferred their social emphasis from the steppe to the oases. The decay and fall of the Mongol empires, and concurrently the weakening political power among the steppe peoples, thereupon gave Islam an opportunity to dominate the oases world.[62]

Theoretically, Qubilai's rule extended overall the vast domains in Asia and Europe occupied by the members of his family. Practically, however, in the sections more remote from China, that suzerainty was little better than nominal and in wide regions it was disputed. Qubilai was the Grand Khan, but time—distances in the huge Empire were so great that the subordinate Qhans who possessed the actual rule on the periphery, especially in Central and Western Asia and eastern Europe, were in practice almost if not entirely, autonomous. During much of the life of Qubilai, moreover, a relative Kaidu, effectively disputed his rule in much of what is now Sinkiang and southern part of Siberia, and for a time invaded Mongolia and threatened Qaraqorum. This resistance ended with his death. But the Chaghatai state, which was established with Chaghatai-Qaidu alliance continued to be ruled by their successors till the emergence of the Barlas Turks in power under Timur.

References

1. *Secret History of the Mongols,* p. 187. Compare with the translation given by R.P. Lister in his, *The Secret History of Genghis Khan,* "What will happen in your dealings with each other, you two? Mother Earth is wide. I will give you the rule over grazing grounds distant the one from the other. You must keep your word, and give the people no cause for ridicule," p. 200.
2. *History of the World Conqueror,* p. 271.
3. *Janiut Tawarikh,* p. 145.
4. *Tarikh-i-Rashidi,* pp. 30-31.
5. Stanley Lane-Poole, *The Mohammadan Dynasties,* New York, Republished, 1965, p. 241.
6. *The Venture of Islam,* p. 410.
7. *Cathay and the way thither,* p. 160.
8. Bertold Spular, *The Mongols in History,* p. 57
9. *Four studies,* i, pp. 112-13.
10. *New Encyclopedia Britannica,* xv, p. 709.
11. *Secret History of the Mongols,* p. 167.
12. Ibid., pp. 183-86.
13. Ibid., p. 191-92.
14. Ibid., p. 200-201.
15. *Jamiut Tawaikh,* pp. 147-49.
16. *Secret History of the Mongols,* pp. 202.
17. Ibid., pp. 206-7 and 209.
18. Ibid., pp. 215-16.
19. *Medieval Researches,* i, p. 69
20. *History of the World Conqueror,* pp. 271-73. For his earlier career we are informed by Juvaini, that he was assigned the administration of the *Yasa* and the law, both the enforcement there of and the reprimanding and Chastisement of those that contravened it (p.40). Rashiduddin writes, "And whoever wishes to have a good knowledge of the *yosun,* manners, and *biligs,* let him go to Chaghatai. At another place he writes, "that his father Chingiz Khan said to the emirs. "Whoever wishes to learn the *yasa* and *yosum* of kingship should follow Chaghatai," p.18 and n.145).
21. *The March of the Barbarians,* p. 96.

22. *Jamiut Tawaikh,* p. 85
23. Ibid., pp. 46, 83.
24. Ibid., pp. 124-28. In between, the Mongols came to Bamiyan where Metiken, second son of Chaghatai and favourite of Chingiz Khan was killed. After the massacre the city was given the name of Ma'u-Baligh (Bad Town). This event fell out in the year 618/1221-22. See *History of the World Conqueror,* pp. 132-33. Rashiduddin says that the city was named Ma'u Qurghan (Bad Fortress) and further informs that Chingiz Khan was greatly distressed on this account. When Chaghatai arrived, Chingiz Khan gave orders that no one was to tell him of his son's death, and far several days he would say that Mo'etuken had gone to such-and-such a place. Then one day, he purposely picked a quarrel with his sons and said: "You do not listen to my words and have ignored what I told you." Chaghatai knelt down and said: "We shall act as the Khan commands and if we fall short may we die!" Chingiz several times repeated this question: "Is it true what thou sayest and wilt thou keep they word?" He answered: "If I disobey and do not keep my word, may I die!" Chingiz Khan then said: "Mo'etuken is dead, and thou must not weep and lament." Fire fell into Chaghatai's bowels, but obeying his father's command he exercised forbearance and did not weep. After a while he went out on the pretext of some necessity and wept in secret in a corner for a moment or two. Then wiping his eyes, he returned to his father. See *Jamiut Tawarikh,* pp. 137-38.
25. *History of the World Conqueror,* p. 136.
26. Ibid., p. 140.
27. Ibid., p. 187.
28. Ibid., p. 191.
29. Michael Prawdin, p. 405.
30. Hamby Gavin, pp. 127-28.
31. H.A.R. Gibb, p. 570.
32. *Jamiut Tawarikh,* p. 149 and 37n.
33. *History of the World Conqueror,* p. 273. Rashiduddin gives eight. See *Jamiut Tawarikh,* p. 135.
34. *Jamiut Tawarikh,* p. 149.
35. *History of the World Conqueror,* p. 273-74.
36. *Jamiut Tawarikh,* p. 149.
37. *History of the World Conqueror,* p. 274.
38. *Jamiut Tawarikh,* pp. 149-50.
39. *History of World Conqueror,* p. 276-76.
40. *Jamiut Tawarikh,* pp. 150, 345.
41. Ibid., pp. 138-39, 254 and 262. Abishqa had served under Mongke Qa'an during his campaign against ther uler of Khitar, p. 224.
42. Ibid., pp. 252-53.
43. Rashiduddin at a place gives the list of the supporters of Ariq Boke

which consisted of Orqina, Asutai and Urung-Tash sons of Mongke Qa'an, Alghu and others. See *Jamiut Tawarikh,* p. 251. On the struggle between Qaidu and Ariq Boke see Peter Jackson,'Dissolusion'; Rossabi, *Khubilai Khan,* pp. 153-62 and Michal Biran, *Qaidu,* 21. Leo de Hartog mentions that Hulegu Khan supported Qubilai and Berke sided with Ariq Boke, see *Russia and the Mongol Yoke,* p. 61. Also see *Jamiut Tawarikh,* p. 253.
44. *Jamiut Tawarikh,* pp. 143-44, 150.
45. Ibid., pp. 150-51.
46. Ibid., pp. 153-54.
47. Ibid., pp. 254-57.
48. Ibid., pp. 257-61. Earlier it has been mentioned that Alghu died in the year 662/1263 (p. 151).
49. Ibid., p. 139.
50. Ibid., pp. 142-43.
51. Ibid., p. 151.
52. Ibid., pp. 139-40.
53. *New Encyclopaedia of Islam,* xv, p. 811.
54. *Mongols, Turks and Others,* pp. 321-22.
55. Michael Prawdin, p. 246.
56. Ibid, p. 255-57, 261, 293, 320.
57. *Qaidu and the Rise of the Independent Mongol State in Central Asia,* p. 1.
58. *Medieval Researches,* ii, p. 9.
59. *Turkestan Down to the Mongol Invasion,,* V, p. 490.
60. *Qaidu and the Rise of the Independdent State,* p. 1.
61. *Comprehensive History of India,* V, p. 98.
62. Owen Lattimore, *Inner Asian Frontiers of China* (Oxford, 1988), p. 180.

4

Relations with China

As noted earlier, Qaidu was the first of his family openly to defy imperial authority. In 1256 he had arrested and then refused to return to the court an envoy sent to him by the Khaqan. Mongke, presumably pre-occupied with the approaching campaign against the Sung, took no action against the rebellious prince. Then, when the struggle for the succession between Qubilai and Arigh Boke broke out, Khaidu did what he could to encourage the conflict, hoping of course, to bring about the ruin of the house of the Toluids.[1] The war lasted for four year from 1260 to 1264.[2]

As soon as the Chaghatai Khanate became stable and organized, Qaidu opened hostility with great Khan, ubilai in China. It involved a mighty opposition who could challenge and stake the claim over the Mongolian thronc. Qubilai was not only a Mongol but also a member of the royal family, a grandson of the great Khan Uktae. Since Central Asia shared a common frontier with Kubilai's domains, the hostility could result threatening the border- lands in northwest China. This could not only an infliction on Chinese peasants but to hamper the long-distance caravan trade across Eurasia that Qubilai sought to foster and that required secure towns and oases in Central Asia. If the hostile groups of the Central Asian Khanate controlled these essential halting places, they could disrupt the commerce.[3] Even more threatening was the proximity of Central Asia to Mongolia, the traditional homeland of the Mongols. For Kubilai Khan to abandon his native territories was unthinkable. In addition, Central Asia was vital to Kubilai's grandiose plans for long-distance trade. It was the crossroads in commerce between China and India, the Middle East and Europe. Caravans transporting goods across Eurasia counted on stops in the towns and oases of Central Asia both to trade with the local inhabitants and to replenish their supplies. These halting places were essential for the survival of the caravan trade. Similarly, the towns and oases needed the farming enclaves nearby for their food and supply.[4]

The precise date for the onset of hostilities between Kubilai Khan and Qaidu is difficult to establish. However, according to Polo. "In Turkestan there is a king called Kaidu, who is nephew to the Great Khan. For he was son of Ogedei, who was the Great Khan's brother german. He has many cities and towns under his sway and is a very great lord. He is a Tartar and so are his people. They are good fighting men. And no wonder; for they are all inured to war. I assure you that Kaidu is never at peace with the Great Khan, but maintains constant war fare against him."[5]

Polo assigns the reason to this conflict the share of the conquests made by his father particularly a part of the provinces of Cathay and Manzi. The Great Khan was willing to give the share provided Kaidu should be obedient like other barons and present himself in the later's court. But Kaidu did not trust his uncle and declined to go. He professed himself ready to be obedient where he was; but he would not go to the Great Khan's court for anything in the world, because he feared for his life. This was the beginning of the quarrel between the two. And from it sprang a great war and many a fiercely fought battle. All the year long the Great Khan kept his armies all round Kaidu's dominions, so that neither Kaidu nor his men should do any harm to his land or his subjects. But King Qaidu, for all the Great Khan's armies, had not ceased from incursions into his territory and fought several engagements with forces that attacked him. According to Polo, Qaidu could muster the strength of about 100,00 horsemen in the field who were all seasoned warriors inured to warfare and battle. In addition he had with him several barons of the imperial lineage that is of the linkage of Chinghiz Khan.[6]

Qaidu represented the Mongolian nomadic values that threatened the increasingly sedentary Mongolian dynasty in China. He enjoyed the life of a nomad and lord of pastoral herdsmen, not the life of the governor or ruler of peasantry. His habitat was the open spaces, not a grand palace in a populous capital city. He favoured the pastoral nomadic society rather than the sedentary agricultural society ruled by a Central Government and staffed by a bureaucracy. The Chinese sources portray Qaidu as a plunderer and treacherous renegade. But he did not intend either to destroy the flourishing town in the region or to dismantle their commercial bases. But he was the undisputed leader among Uktae's and Chaghatai's surviving descendants. Basing his power upon Jungaria and the Semirechie he had expelled Qubilai's representatives from Kashghar, Yarkand and Khotan by 1273 and in 1276 was threatening the Turfa-Kucha region. Recognizing the gravity of the situation, Qubilai soon reasserted his authority in the Tarimbasin but in 1277 Qaidu captured Qaraqorum, supported by Mongol chieftains who resented Qubalai's policy of sinification. In 1278 Qubilai's best general Bayan (Marce Polo's Bayan of hundred eyes) invaded Mongolia and recaptured Karakorum but Qaidu retained control of Jungaria and continued to raid Mongolia with impunity severing the entire lives of communication—which was why Marco Polo travelled by sea when he conducted an imperial princess from China to Iran in the late 1280s. Qubalai's pre-occupations with his Indo-Chinese and naval expeditions prevented him from launching a decisive attack upon Qaidu, who enjoyed the strategic advantage of control over the Chinese marches where he could recruit followers from among the same warlike tribes, which had won Chingiz's empire for him. His career was proof of Qubilai's lack of foresight in withdrawing court and government from Mongolia, thereby severing his family's personal links with the Mongol and Turkish tribes upon whose loyalty the survival of the empire depended. Qaidu's death removed the most formidable threat to the Yuan dynasty until its expulsion from China by the Mings over sixty years later. In fact, Qaidu actively discouraged the pillaging of the Central Asian oases and must have instructed his underlings not to harass their inhabitants. Instead, the taxes levied on the towns and the revenues he derived were used to support his forces. Nonetheless, he appeared to be the defender of the Mongolian heritage that, in his view Qubilai Khan had betrayed.[7]

On 9 July 1266, Qubilai had appointed his own son Nomukhan as *pei ping wang* (prince of the pacification of the north), intending that the young man take charge of the military affairs of North China and prevent incursions onto the soil of northwest China. Yet five years elapsed before Qubilai actually assigned his son to the Central Asian outpost of Almalikh (modern Huo-cheng, Sinkiang) to protect that region from Qaidu's incursions. Qubalai also made a mistake grievously in sending several cousins of Nomukhan's to accompany him for they all engaged in bitter disputes that impeded the expeditions and finally led to its failure. It seems that Qaidu had organized a coalition of Mongolian princes in Central Asia that contested Qubilai and his successors.[8]

Nomukhan made little progress in crushing the dissidents in Central Asia. He succeeded in developing supply lines for his troops, but could not readily engage the enemy. Qaidu's forces organized guerilla—like operations against his troops but would not fight traditional battle. Whenever they found themselves outnumbered or in distress, they simply fled into the steppe lands of desert, trerrain with which they were familiar. Nomukhan's forces were frustrated because they could not easily pursue the highly mobile guerrilla forces and engage them in combat. To break the deadlock, in 1275 Qubilai sent his wife's nephew An-tung (1245-93), a capable and prominent figure who was at that time right prime minister to assist Nomukhan. On arriving Nomukhan's encampment, An-tung quickly recognized that factionalism divided the various princes on the expedition and was hampering effective operations. By siding with Nomukhan, however, he too became embroiled in these disputes.[9]

In late 1276, the princes who accompanied Nomukhan plotted to sabotage his expedition. The conspirators, who included two of Arigh Boke's sons and one of Mongke's sons, seized Nomukhan and delivered him to the Khan of the Golden Horde of Russia and turned over An-tung to Qaidu. Their captors detained the two men for almost a decade but did not harm them. The conspirators were disappointed, however, to discover that Qaidu equivocated on an alliance with them; he did not want them in his domains. Shortly thereafter, they migrated to what they perceived to be a safer location, the Mongolian steppe. Eventually, both the Khans of the Golden Horde and Qaidu unable to raise a ransom for the two captives and seeing no gain from continuing to detain them released Nomukhan and An-tung. Khubilai warmly greeted his son and his nephew when they returned in 1284 and once against granted them their old positions and titles.

Qubilai had not been idle during the decade that elapsed between the seizure and release of Nomukhan and An-tung. On learning of the capture of Nomkhan, he had dispatched Bayan, his ablest and most renowned general to retrieve his son. Bayan, who had just returned from his extremely successful campaigns against the Southern Sung dynasty, was repeatedly frustrated in his efforts. Like Nomukhan himself, Bayan was unable to engage the enemy, as Qaidu's forces continually eluded his troops. Nomukhan's leaderless troops also made some valiant attempts to free Qubilai's son but they too failed to secure his release.[10]

Qubilai eventually acknowledged that he could not control Central Asia and was compelled to accept Qaidu as the defacto ruler of the area. Even his most prominent general had been unable to extend Qubiliai's suzerainty into Central Asia. Admitting his failure, he reluctantly relinquished his position in the steppe lands and oasis of the region. He retreated to the more defensible confines of Chinese settlement, allowing Qaidu free rein beyond these villages. Yet he could not prevent Qaidu from raiding these villages, which had been his primary objective. The difficulties he encountered were that the supply lines required to maintain his armies and the friendly local in habitants were long and fragile; that the constant harassment and elusiveness of the nomads irritated and intimidated his soldiers and allies alike; and that the self-sufficiency he sought to achieve for the oases and towns in the regions was never realized. In short, Khubilai's foray into Central Asia had achieved nothing.[11]

We find Qaidu allying with a Mongolian commander Nayan who rebelled in Manchuria. However, Nayan was defeated by Qubilai himself and was executed. According to Marco Polo Qubilai's forces consisted of 46,000 men.[12]

After Qubalai's death his grandson and successor, Temur (1294-1307), supported by the veteran Bayan resolutely upheld his position as Khaqan, checked Qaidu's ambitions and reasserted his primacy over the western Khanates by vigorous diplomacy. His successor however, had little influence over the course of events in Central Asia.[13]

The last battle between the Yuan army and Qaidu allied with Dua Khan took place at Tieh-Chien-ku and Khara Khada (Ho-La ho-ta) of the Altai Mountains in September 1301 when Qaidu and Dawa launched their last offensive. The encounter itself was perhaps inconclusive, as the Chinese and Persian sources contradict each other about its results.[14]

What was important was its indirect results, for Dua was wounded in the battle and Qaidu died soon thereafter perhaps of a wound he had suffered. It is considered among the greatest achievements of Temur Khakan to have achieved successful concluding of protected and costly war with Khaidu and Dua. This achievement, however, did not come easily. Despite Qubilai's continual efforts for a quarter of a century to strangle his Central Asian enemies by denying to them the food-producing sedentary areas, Qaidu and Dua still remained resilient at the time of Qubilai's death, extending their control over Uighuristan and frequently invading Mongolia.[15]

With the death of Qaidu, the main stumbling block to peace among the Mongolian Khanates was removed. It was Dua, Qaidu's ally, who took the initiative for peace. Tired of his hopeless challenges to the authority of the Khakan and more concerned with establishing his own supremacy in Central Asia, Dua first manipulated to have Ogedei's son Chapar to succeed Qaidu as the ruler of the Ogedei Khanate in the summer of 1303. Then in the fall of the same year he persuaded Chapar to join him in proposing to Temur that they cease their hostilities, making known their willingness to recognize Temur's authority as the Khakan of all Mongols.[16]

Temur responded to this proposal quickly and favourably. Though a *quriltai* for peace, as was proposed by Dua, was never held, an agreement on the cessation of war was nevertheless achieved. A mission sent jointly by Temur, Dua and Chapar arrived at the court of Ilkhan Oljaitu (1304-16) in early 1304, seeking the latter's agreement to the peace proposal and the re-establishment of unity among all Mongols. Though the peace achieved in 1303 was short-lived, it not only reestablished the nominal suzerainty of the Yuan over the Mongolian Khanates, but it also gave the Yuan the opportunity to remove permanently the threat from Central

Asia by separating the heirs of Chaghatai from those of Ogedei. Dua and Chapar soon clashed with each other over the question of territory. In this conflict Temur backed Dua, and in the fall of 1306 he sent an army commanded by Khaishan across the southern Altai to his aid. Attacking Chapar's forces from the rear, Khaishan captured several members of Chapar's family and advanced as far as Irtysh River. Chapar had no choice but to surrender to Dua. Chapar was, later dethroned by Dua, probably in 1307 and his younger brother Yangichar was established by Dua as a puppet Khan of Ogodei's *ulus*. Forced by circumstances, Chapar surrendered to the Yuan in 1310 during Khaishan's reign, thus making the end of the Ogodei's *ulus* that had challenged the Yuan on the battlefield nearly forty years. The Ogodeid lands south and west of the Altai mountains were taken by the Yuan dynasty, whereas most of the remaining Ogodeid territory was annexed to the Chaghadaid Khanate.[17]

The new borders created a problem of pasture lands—Esan Boga, the Chaghatai Khan (*c.*1310-18) had sent envoys and gifts to Tughaji Jinsank, the grand marshal of the Yuan garrisons, asking to readjust the summer and winter pastures. He headed twelve tumens of Yuan soldiers and was stationed on the Esen Muren, one of the upper reaches of the Irtish river, and in Qobaq, the center of the original Ogodeid appanage over which he took after Chapar's surrender. This place was later a major station for the commercial embassies going from Central Asia to China. The negotiations, however, did not go well on the question of *Yarligh* issued by Esan Boga, since issuing *Yarligh* was right of the Yuan.[18]

Another reason for the tension between the Yuan and the Chaghadaids was the volume of trade going on the borders. *Yuan shi* reports that during 1312-13 Esen Boqa sent several tributes of jewelry, furs, horses, camels, jades and wine to the Yuan court and was generously rewarded. But the traffic to and from Central Asia and the Central Asian embassies in particular had become a burden on the Yuan court, since it was the duty on the part of Yuan to maintain the post stations (*jam*) in which these missions lodged on their way. A major reason for the deterioration of the relations between the Chaghadaids and the Yuan at this stage has been suggested the Chaghadaid' fear of joint Yuan-Ilkhanid attack. The idea was raised by Abishqa, Yuan emissary to the Ilkhanid. While passing through the Chaghadaid domains, Abishqa, perhaps out of drunkenness, claimed he knew secrets that would interest Esen Boqa. He also indicated that the Yuan forces had already begun to move towards Chaghadaids. Esen Boqa blocked the diplomatic traffic between the Yuan and the Ilkhanate and detained these groups of envoys during 1313-14. The messengers were sent to Kashghar and their horses and property were confiscated. Esen Boqa tried to ally with Ozbeg, the newly enthroned Khan of the Golden Horde (1313-41) as a counterweight against the alleged Yuan-Ilkhanid coalition. But the superiority of the Yuan could not be lessened. As after few skirmishes and the surrender of Qaidu's son, Orus, to the Yuan in 1320, Chaghadaids remained subordinates to the Yuan. Later in the period of Kebek, the relations improved and the annual tribute from Central Asia to China restored. In 1325, Kebek also received two ladies of the court to marry. These peaceful tributary relations continued also under Kebek's successors. Yuan preserved its supremacy as the representative of the great Khan vis-č-vis the other Khanates. It has been suggested in a recent study that in the second or third decades of the fourteenth centuries Yuan garrisons were stalled enough in nomadic warfare to convince the Central Asian Mongols to seek peace.[19] But it needs further investigations, as we know that the Burlas Turks had become very powerful in Central Asia.

References

1. *Cambridge History of China,* vi, pp. 412. Also Hambly Gavin, pp. 106-7.
2. *China under the Mongol Rule,* p. 278.
3. *Cambridge History of China,* vi, pp. 442-43.
4. *Khubilai Khan,* p. 104.
5. Polo, p. 187.
6. Ibid., p. 287-88.
7. *Cambridge History of China,* p. 443.
8. *China under the Mongol,* p. 412. Also see Hambly Gavin, pp. 106-7.
9. *Khubilai Khan,* pp. 443-44.
10. Ibid., p. 443.
11. Ibid., pp. 444-45.
12. *Cambridge History of China,* vi, pp. 487-88 and Marco Polo, p. 289 and *Khubilai Khan,* pp. 223-24.
13. Hambly Gavin, p. 107.
14. Ibid., vi, pp. 502-3.
15. Ibid., pp. 501-2 and *East Asia: The Great Tradition,* p. 273.
16. *Cambridge History of China,* vi, p. 503.
17. Ibid., pp. 503-4. Also see Liu Yingshay, 'War and peace between the Yuan Dynasty and the Chaghadaid Khanate (1312-23), in *Mongols, Turks and Others,* p. 340.
18. *Liu Yingshang,* op.cit., pp. 341-42.
19. Ibid., pp. 342-54.

5

Indian Campaigns

THE POLITICAL UPHEAVAL IN Central Asia had always caused great concern for India. Before the rise of the Mongols, the Khwarizmian Empire had, touched the Indian frontier. The Turks had already established their rule over northern India, when Mongols were preparing to destroy the Khwarizmian Empire. We learn from Minhaj that Sultan Muhammad Khwarizm Shah became curious to know about the Mongol power in China, sent an embassy to Chinghiz Khan, headed by one Bahauddin Razi. The envoys reached in the presence of Chinghiz Khan who said, "Behold, my affairs and my sovereignty have attained to such a pitch of grandeur that the monarch of the (empire of the) setting sun has sent envoys unto me . . . he requested that the envoys, on both sides, and merchants and caravans, should constantly come and go, and bring and take away with them choice descriptions of arms, clothes, and stuffs and other articles of value and elegance of both empires; and that between the two monarch permanent treaty should be maintained."[1]

Chinghiz Khan dispatched merchants along with the envoys of Sultan Muhammed, about five hundred camel-loads of gold, silver, silks and *targhu* (a description of woven silk of a red colour) together with other precious and valuable commodities that they might trade with them. They entered the territory, according to the chroniclers of Islam by way of Otrar. At that place there was a governor named Kadr Khan who was sent to Sultan Muhammad Shah respecting the importance and value of the merchandise and solicited permission from him, in a perfidious manner, to stop the party of merchants. Having obtained permission to do so, he seized the envoys and the whole of the merchants, and slew them, and took possession of all their property, and sent it to the Sultan's presence. Of that party, there was one person, a camel-driver, who had gone to one of the (public) hot baths, and succeeded in making his escape by way of the fire- place. He having taken to the wilds, returned back to Chin, and made Chinghiz Khan acquainted with the perfidious conduct of Kadr Khan of Otrar and the slaughter of the party.[2]

Chinghiz Khan prepared to take revenge and he caused the forces of Chin and Turkistan to be got ready for that purpose. The fortress and city of Utrar was taken and the whole of the inhabitants were killed.[3] From Utrar, the forces of Chinghiz Khan marched towards Bukhara, captured the city and put the whole population to death. The city of Samarkand also met the same fate. Muhammad Shah was pursued till he died on the way due to a disease. The whole regions of Khwarizm and Khurasan, were traversed by the Mongols.[4]

The Mongols pursued his more valiant son and the crown prince Jalaluddin Mangbarni who fled towards Ghazni, encountered the Mongol upon three different times, and on all three occasions succeeded with the victory. Hearing this Chinghiz himself marched towards Ghazni. Jalaluddin was given a defeat and was compelled to overthrow himself into the river Indus and after crossing it, entered the Indian territories. According to Minhaj, Iltutimash dispatched a force against him upon which Jalaluddin turned aside and proceeded towards Uch and Multan. From there he entered the territory of Kirman and afterwards Fars. On several occasions he defeated the Mongols but could not get rid of them and continued to be persued.[5]

The account of Juvaini is little different from Minhaj. Juvaini informs us that when the news of defeat of the Mongols reached Chinghiz Khan, he immediately reached Ghazni. By that time Jalaluddin had already left Ghazni with the object of crossing the Indus. Chinghiz pursued him, the Mongol army cut off the Sultan's front and rear and encompassed him on every side. Chinghiz Khan commanded his men to exceed themselves in battle and to endeavour to take the Sultan alive. Meanwhile Chaghatai and Ogetei also had arrived from Khwarizm. Jalaluddin continued to fight like an angry lion. The Mongols failed to take him prisoner and he jumped into the river. Chinghiz Khan then prevented the Mongols to catch him. From excess of astonishment he put his hand to his mouth and kept saying to his sons, "Such a son must a father have". Briefly, all of Jalaluddin army that was not drowned in the river were slain by the sword. This event fell out in Rajab of the year 618 (August-September, 1221).[6]

It has been opined that for sometime Chinghiz Khan apparently weighed the possibilities of continuing his campaign farther south and of conquering India. Both he and his advisers realized, however, the tremendous difficulties of such an undertaking and especially of crossing the high mountain ranges. Elin Chu-tsai, among others, strongly advised against the campaign. Finally the Mongol emperor decided to abandon the idea and turned his army back.[7] Chinghiz Khan decided to return from Peshawar to his original home and the reason for his haste to return was that the Khitayans and the Tangut, were profiting by his absence, had grown restive and wavered between submission and insurrection.[8] Minhaj goes further and states that the territories of Chin, Tamghaj and Tingit were in state of revolt and that on account of the very great distance (of the Chinghiz Khan from the scene) , those kingdoms were about to pass out of the hands of the Mughal governors. Chinghiz Khan, on account of this information, became anxious in mind and he consequently set out on his return by way of Lob and the country of Tibbat.[9]

The Secret History of the Mongols gives a different versions and briefly states that Chinghiz Khan pursued Jalaluddin as far as the land of Hindus. There he lost Jalaluddin (even though) he searched as far as the heart of the land of the Hindus he was unable (to find him). Returning, he plundered the people on the edge (of the Hindus' territory) and, taking many camels and many castrated goats, came back. "Then Chinggis Qahan" says *Secret History,* "returned (to his own land), spending the summer on the way on Erdish (Irtysh) river. . . ."[10]

However, when Chaghatai returned without having found Jalaluddin, Chinghiz Khan deputed Torbei Toqshin, together with two *tumen* of Mongol troops to cross the Indus in his pursuit. He took Nandana and turned against Multan. The town of Multan was on the point of surrendering but the heat prevented him to stay further. Having plundered and massacred throughout the province of Multan and Lahore he returned from thence and re-crossed the Indus; and arriving in Ghazna followed in the wake of Chinghiz Khan.[11] Yeme and Subetei, the chief commanders were now sent against Jalaluddin who was near Tirmiz. On their way the Mongols got submission of the people of Balkh, Zava, (the modern Turbat-i-Haidari in Eastern Khorasan) , Nishapur, Mazandran, Damghan and Ray. At Ray they knew about Jalaluddin's flight in the direction of Hamadan, which had submitted before the Mongols and accepted a Mongol *shahna.* They plundered throughout the greater part of Iraq and proceeded towards Ardabil, which they took by siege, slaughtering the inhabitants and pillaging their possessions.[12]

About the death of Jalaluddin there are different accounts. Some believed that, he was killed by a group of the Kurds. The rumours of his being alive rose from time to time. Even a man claiming to Jalaluddin rose in rebellion in the year

633/1235-36 who was put to death by the Mongols. In the year 652/1254-55 again a party of merchants came to the bank of the river Oxus. One of them told the boatmen that he was Sultan Jalaluddin. "To be brief, all those rumours and reports were of no avail," writes Juvaini.[13] Minhaj seems to be sure that he was killed by some chieftains in the territory of Akhlal in Armenia.[14]

About Jalaluddin's asking a place in Delhi from Iltutmish, Juvaini reports that he was denied any support or help, he excused himself from providing a place of abode on the grounds that "nowhere in that region was there a suitable climate nor any locality such as would be fit for a king". When this message reached the Sultan, he turned back and went to the region of Balala and Nikala, where he gathered his supporters and army and ravaged the Jud hills and asked the Khokhar chief to give his daughter to him in marriage.[15]

Regarding Chinghiz Khan's returning back Chin via Koh-i-Karachal, Kamrud he sought permission from Iltutmish.[16] According to Raverty the object of Chinghiz Khan was to save distance and reach Tingkut by the shortest route. By Lakhanawati and Kamrud the distance would have been still lessened. "Chinghiz Khan wintered about the sources of the Indus", which are in Tibbat itself. If so, he would have been very near to Tingkut. He found, however, that he was not likely to obtain the consent of Sultan Iltutimash to take the Karachal routes and as the time pressed he had to give it up and get into the route by which he had entered Khurasan in the outset.[17] While comparing their campaigns in Europe and Syria with India it has been suggested that there was an additional factor of insufficient pasture- land. In Western Europe, and even in Hungary, there were not enough pastures for the Mongol cavalry and stock. India too, was unsuited climatically and geographically for Mongol style of nomadism.[18]

A recent study made by a cultural anthropologist suggests that the Mongol conquest stopped at the city of Multan in the summer of 1221, the Year of the Horse. After descending from the mountains of Afghanistan onto the plains of the Indus River earlier that year, Chinghiz Khan had considered conquering all of northern India, circling around south of the Himalayas and heading north across the Sung territory of China. Such a plan suited the Mongol sensibility that one should never return by exactly the same route that one came. However, the geography and climate stopped him. As soon as the Mongols left the dry and colder region of the mountains, both warriors and horses weakened and grew sick. Even more alarming, the Mongol bows that were so well adapted to the extreme cold and heat of the steppe homeland also weakened in the damp and seemed to lose the powerful accuracy that made the Mongol warrior such a dreaded shot. Facing these obstacles, Chinghiz Khan headed back into the mountains in February and despite the tremendous loss of lives among the prisoners who cleared the snow filled the passes, he took his army to more comfortable and colder terrain. He left behind two *tumen*, some twenty thousand men, to continue the India campaign, but by summer illness and heat had so depleted their ranks that the survivors withdrew and limped back to the benign and healthful environment of Afghanistan.[19]

Juvaini gives briefly about Jalaududdin Mangbarni's adventures in India. He writes, "when the Sultan had escaped from the twin dangers of water and fire, that is the flood of the Indus and the flame of the fury of Chinghiz Khan, he was joined by five or six of his guards (*mufradan*) whom Fate had not destroyed nor the blast from the flames of tribulation and calamity confided to the dust of annihilation". He further informs that after defeating a band of Indians, he was able to gather good number of horses and arms. . . . Re-equipped his forces . . . until the number reached three or four thousands men. Chinghiz Khan who was in Ghazni, hearing the news of his gathering forces sent an army of the Mongols under Torbei Toqshin who crossed the Indus, the sultan, not being strong enough to oppose them set out in the direction of Delhi. The Mongols, for their part, upon hearing the news of his flight, turned back and laid waste the districts of Malikfur (in Rawalpindi district).[20] At another place Juvaini writes that the great heat of the climate prevented the Mongols remaining longer; so having plundered and massacred throughout the province of Multan and Lahore they returned from thence and re-crossed the Indus; and arriving in Ghazna followed in the wake of Chinghiz Khan.[21]

After getting no response from Iltutmish, Jalaluddin returned back to the regions of Balala and Nikala (in the vicinity of Lahore). Here refugees from the various armies gathered round him from all sides. . . . Number reached 10000 men. Juvaini speaks about his matrimonial relations with the Khokhas chief who gave his daughter to the Sultan in marriage. Mangbarni sent forces to defeat Nasiruddin Qabacha, the enemy of the Khokhars. . . . Qubacha fled from Uch to Multan. Jalaluddin, however, due to the hot weather left for Jud hills and Balala and Nikala. On the way he took the possession of the castle of Parasravar (in Sialkot district). Mongols forces were after him, hence he left the Indian frontier and reached Persia, Georgia, Rum . . . till he died.[22]

Before leaving, Indian frontier region, Jalaluddin left some of his nobles, in possession of the territories, which he seized during his stay. Wafa Malik was entrusted with the administration of Baniyan and some parts of Ghazni, such as Nangrahar, Kurram and Furshur, which were still outside the Mongol control. Jahan Pahlwan was posted in the fort of Nandanah in the Koh-i-Jud area. Both of them continued to retain their hold over these Indian territories for a quite a long time. It seems that after defeating Qabacha in AD 1228, Iltutmish acquired control over Sind and Panjab and consequently made an expedition into the Koh-i-Jud and Baniyan territories. Jahan Pahlwan was driven away while Wafa Malik retain Baniyan by paying allegiance to Iltutimash. Minhaj includes Kujah, Nandanah and Sialkot in the list of

Iltutmish's conquests.[23]

The situation remained unchanged till AD 1235 when the Mongols threatened the Qarlughs and appeared with a large army headed by their general one Hoqutar who had already plundered Kashmir and made a large number of people captives.[24] Hasan Qarlugh seems to have acknowledged the suzerainty of the Mongol emperor Ogedei and pledged to pay an annual tribute to him. The situation created by the Mongols compelled Iltutimash to march against the Qarlugh and he took the royal armies towards Baniyan. He fell seriously ill on his way and was then brought back to his capital, shortly afterwards he passed away in AD 1236.[25]

Soon after the death of Iltutmash, Wafa Malik succeeded in capturing the fort of Nandanah and established his control over the entire tract of the Koh-i-Jud. He assumd the royal title of Saif ul-Duniya-wa'l-Din Abu'l Muzaffar al-Hasan Qarlugh and minted the coins in his name.[26] He also stopped paying tribute to the Mongols which caused a Mongol invasion in AD 1238. The Mongols under Nuin Nikudar deprived him of his territories obliging him to flee towards Multan and Sind. He sent his eldest son to the court of Razia in Delhi. She received him with distinction and assigned him the *vilayat* of Baran to his charge.[27]

Gaining possession over Qarlugh's territories, the Mongols now planned to invade India. They marched under Bahadur Tair from Ghur and arrived on the river Indus. Kabir Khan-i-Ayaz, the *muqta* of Multan prepared to give a battle to the Mongols, who without fighting him retired towards Lahore. It appears that the Mongols were led by the leaders of the second rank and their troops consisted the contingents of those Muslim and petty rulers who had submitted to them in those parts.[28] Lahore was not prepared for a battle and the *muqta* of the city Malik Karakash left for Delhi. The Mongols captured Lahore, but on the next day after its capture Ogedei Khan died. It perhaps made them to retire but only after destroying the city. It was occupied by the

Khokhars after the departure of the Mongols.[29]

After the death of Ogedei Khan the throne of the Mongol Khan remained vacant for nearly four years. This gave an opportunity to Hasan Qarlugh to recover his lost terrirtories from the Mongols and his son also joined him. Kabir Khan-i-Ayaz had also died in 1241 and was succeeded by his son Tajuddin in Sind. The Qarlughian armies could take Multan later after the death of Tajuddin and became the masters of the whole region in the northwest frontier except the Kohi-i-Jud which had became the center of the Khokhars' activities. It seems that the The Khokhars had joined hands with the Mongols and acted as their guide during their future campaigns in India in AD 1245 under Mangutah.[30]

Subsequent events reveal that Hasan Qarlugh must have patched up his differences with the Mongols and have accepted a Mongol *shahnah* at his court. Hasan Qarlugh made attack on Multan, though killed in the battle, the Qarlughian armies were successful in getting Multan from Malik Kishlu on the false situation by keeping news of Hasan's death as a secret.[31]

After the death of Hasan Qarlugh, his eldest son Nasiruddin Muhammad succeeded as the ruler of Bamiyan and Koh-i-Jud regions. He acted with patience and shrewdness in maintaining diplomatic ties with his Mongol suzerain and followed a pragmatic policy towards the Sultans of Delhi. It looks that he had created conducive conditions in the region for smooth flow of trading activities and used to levy certain taxes at border posts to make himself, economically, strong. The abundance of coins found in salt range districts points to a brisk trade carried on by the merchant caravans between India, Iran and Central Asia through this region.[32]

In the meantime many of the frontier governors had become independent and began to assert their authority in the court also. They proved disloyal to the court and few were defiant enough to visit the courts of the Mongols. It has rightly been suggested that before the liberation of the territories of Lahore, Jullunder, Multan and upper-Sind, Ulugh Khan, the then de-facto ruler of Delhi had entered into a secret alliance with the Qarlughs in 1258 and with the latter's help also concluded a no-war pact with Hulegu in 1259. Ulugh Khan followed the policy of non-interference towards the Mongol vassals of Lahore and Multan for sometime. No sooner the civil war started in the Mongol Empire than he seized these territories. He also did not support Qarlugh ruler against the Mongols who suspected him of foul play. Hulegu summoned the Qarlugh ruler to his court and ordered Malik Shamsuddin Kart of Herat to inquire into the matter. Malik Kart dealt with the accused severely and killed him along with some of his officers. After that, the territories of Baniyan and Koh-i-Jud, were brought by the Mongols under their direct control.[33] It is the same period when Chaghatais - Kaidu alliance had resulted their expansion up to Ghazni and had become immediate neighbourers of the Sultans of Delhi.

Returning back to the Mongol activities in India, as noticed earlier, the fort of Nandana was taken by the Mongols after which they appeared at the foot of the city of Multan which was invested for forty two days. According to Minhaj the leader of the Mongols was one Turti. During that contest, Malik Nasiruddin Qabacha opened the door of his treasury and conferred numerous benefits upon the people and showed much proofs of boldness, ability, expertness and courage that the mention thereof will endure upon the pages of time until the judgment day. This affair of the fortress of Multan happened in the year 621 H 1224.[34] Soon afterwards according to a recent study there appeared a second Mongol invasion on the dominions of Qabacha. Measures were taken to defend Multan during its siege by the Mongols who had arrived with great preparations along with a large army with siege equipments, but took to flight after three months. In general during Iltutimash's reign, the

Mongol pressure on the Hindukush and the Indus region served to weaken his rivals Tajuddin Yalduz and Nasiruddin Qabacha. Mongol troops under Chaghatai and Ogedei also ravaged the southern Panjab and Chaghatai spent a winter in Kalanjar. At about the same time an embassy arrived of Berka Khan of the Golden Horde, which had newly converted to Islam.[35] This observation needs to be verified from other researches, as we know that Berka Khan had not yet become the lord of the Golden Horde and ruled between AD 1258-67. Minhaj mentions the embassy of Berka Khan in the year AD 1260.[36]

It was pressure of the Mongols, which obliged number of maliks of Ghur to join Nasiruddin Qabacha. Later a body of the Khalj tribe who were earlier part of the Khwarizmian forces, acquired supremacy over the district of Mansura under their leader Malik Khan, the Khalj. But he was defeated in a battle by Qabacha and was slain.[37] In this same period Minhaj, the author of *Tabakat-i-Nasiri*, reached Uch.[38] After annexing the dominions of Qabacha in the year 1228 Iltutimash and his successors came into the direct contact with the Mongols as they had already established themselves in Afghanistan.[39]

In the Mongol *quriltai* convened for the coronation of Ogedei Khan in 1229, it was decided to re-conquer and annex Khurasan and Afghanistan. This resulted in a series of fresh assaults on the Indian territories. In 1235-36, the principality of Siestan in western Afghanistan was made to acknowledge Mongol sway. At a second *quritlai* in 1235, further Mongol troops under Oqotar were ordered to advance on India, and Kashmir was ravaged in the course of a campaign lasting six months.[40] Across the Helmand, through Baluchistan, Mongol horsemen became active in Derajat valley leading to Upper Sind and finally annexed the territory of Hasan Qarlugh, one of the lieutinent of Jalaluddin Mangbarni who had carved out a principality in the districts, east of the Indus. Professor I.H. Siddiqui has given a detailed account of Qarlugh kingdom founded by Malik Saifa-Din Hasan Qarlugh, entitled Wafa Malik, in AD 1225 which served as a buffer state between the Mongol Empire and the Delhi Sultanate till 1266.[41] Hasan Qarlugh sought help from Razia but of no avail. It pleased the Mongols who like Chinghiz remained neutral in Razia's reign. Following her deposition which the Mongols seem to have construed as terminating the non-aggression pact with Delhi, they decided at last on bringing India within their schemes of conquest.[42]

To repeat, major attack of the Mongols on the Indian territory has been reported in AD 1241, when they invaded Lahore under their leader Bahadur Tair, the commander of the forces in Herat, Ghor, Ghazni and Turkmenistan. The city was under Malik Karakush who fled to Delhi and left the inhabitants at their ill fate. When the Mongols occupied Lahore, the news of Ogedei's death reached which compelled them to return as a custom to elect a new *Khaqan.* Before leaving they destroyed the city. The Khokhars who had their center in the Jud hills came and occupied the city. The sack of Lahore had far-reaching results. The trade route via Lahore was now in the hands of the tribes and the traders had to follow a more southern route via Multan. Minhaj, the author of *Tabakat-i-Nasiri* sent some gifts to his sister in Khurasan via Multan, which was a longer one. The city of Lahore could be recovered and repopulated by Balban but its prosperity could be regained only under the Mughals when it was made a *suba.* However, the Mongols succeeded in pushing back the frontier line of the Sultans of Delhi.[43]

Bahadur Tair was succeeded by Mangutah in Afghanistan. He with the help and guidance from the Khokhars attacked Multan. But the armies from Delhi under Ulugh Khan repelled them and a large number of the Mongols were made captives.[44] Reason for this Mongol invasion has been given the disorganized affairs of the region, as there was no control of the Sultan in this direction.[45] The following year also the Mongols under their leader Nuin Sali Bahadur once again invaded Multan and occupied the city. This time negotiations were opened and the governor Chinghiz Khan agreed to pay an indemnity of 100000 dinars. It is believed that this agreement was made by the intervention of Bahauddin Zakaria, the famous saint of Multan who negotiated with the vassal ruler of Herat Shamsuddin Kurt.[46] After the above agreement Sali Bahadur raised the siege of Multan marched on to Lahore where he imposed the same terms and conditions to the governor who even agreed to be a tributary vassal of the Mongols.[47] It has been suggested that the political settlements following Nasiruddin Mahmud's accession probably kept Ulugh Khan busy in Delhi and no reinforcement could at once be sent to the affected regions.[48] The reason is convincing, as we know the governors in the frontier regions had always been acting their own and were almost independent.[49] In the end of the same year Minhaj mentions an expedition led by Ulugh Khan towards Jud hills to suppress the Khokhars who had guided the Mongols in their last campaign. This operation against the tribes has been connected with the Mongol invasion as Minhaj states that is was to relieve Multan and destroy the "infidels of Chin."[50] On the basis of *Rauzatul-Jinnat* it has been claimed that Shamsuddin's successor, Ruknuddin in Herat controlled the highways "as far as the frontiers of Delhi". And when Lahore is next mentioned in the pages of the *Tabakat-i-Nasiri* under the year 652/1254, it is described as a Mongol dependency.[51]

In the first year of his reign, Sultan Nasiruddin Mahmud Shah marched towards the bank of river Indus for the purpose of destroying the Mongols, crossed the river Ravi and encamped near Sudhara. Ulugh Khan led the army, ravaged the Jud hills and killed the Khokhars in great number.[52] In 648/1250, the fifth year of his reign we hear that Ikhtiyaruddin Kurez from Multan, made a great number of Mongols captive, sent them to the capital and the city of Delhi was decorated for this success, as stated by Minhaj. Raverty has some doubts over this statement.[53]

During the next ten years or so the condition in Panjab remained chaotic. Jalaluddin Masud Shah and Sher Khan, a cousin of Balban had sought the Mongol help and interference in the region so as to oppose the Sultan. However, the affairs improved with the diplomatic steps taken by Balban. In the Mongol kingdoms too there was a tension for some time, hence the situation remained under control. But the region of the northwest frontier and Panjab remained under the influence of the Mongols. The modern scholars are of the view that there had been some understanding between the Delhi and the Mongols, which prevented further inroads of the later for few years. The mutual respect for each other's territories was assured.[54]

With the accession of Balban on the throne a new era started in this direction. He was the first among the Sultans who took seriously the cause of the Mongols. He did not even leave his capital for long as the Mongols had made their inroads an annual feature. When his generals, Adil Khan and Tamar Khan suggested to him the conquest of Gujrat, Malwa and other provinces of Hindustan which had been under the 'sway of Aibak and Iltutimash', Balban thus stated his policy:

"It will not be an act of wisdom to leave Delhi and to go on distant campaigns in these days of turmoil and insecurity when the Mongols have occupied all the lands of Islam, devastated Lahore and made it a point to invade our country once every year. . . . If I move out of the capital, the Mongols are sure to avail themselves of the opportunity by sacking Delhi and ravaging the Doab. Maintaining peace and consolidating our power in our own kingdom is far better than invading foreign territories, while our own kingdom is insecure. Further, the newly-conquered areas will require competent officers and well-equipped armies, which I am unable to spare at the present juncture, I have, therefore, made up my mind to face the Mongols with strong organized forces. . . .'[55]

Early in his reign Balban took an expedition into the Jud hills to suppress the Khokhars who had made the region turbulent and had allied with the Mongols on earlier occasions. Later, he recovered Lahore and rebuilt and repopulated it and made fresh appointment of officers for its administration.[56] To meet the Mongol raids he posted Sher Khan on the Punjab frontier. He was given the charge of Sunam, Bhatinda, Lahore and Dipalpur. Sher Khan rebuilt the fortress of Bhatner and maintained a well-equipped army of several thousand horsemen and by suppressing the Jats, Khokhars and Mandahirs along with Bhattis who inhabited the unregulated regions where he restored some order and control. He effectively checked the Mongols from entering the sultanate territory.[57]

It is after the death of Sher Khan and retiring of Kashlu Khan into Bamiyan that Balban entrusted Sind with Multan as its capital to his eldest son Prince Muhammad and appointed his second son Bughra Khan as the warden of frontier with Sunam and Samana as important outposts. However, the pressure of the Chaghatai Mongols continued on the Punjab border, which at times acquired menacing shape. During this period whenever the Mongol raids are mentioned, it is said that the royal forces obtained victories and drove away the enemies so that they were unable to advance beyond the river Beas.[58]

Around 680/1281-82 Bughra Khan was transferred permanently to Lakhnauti which possibly weakened the frontier defenses in the last years of Balban's reign, since Isami records an invasion by two bands of Mongols in which the force sent to repel them by Prince Muhammad suffered a reverse.[59] A heavier blow was to fall in the winter of 683/1284-85, when Muhammad himself was defeated and killed in battle with the Mongol commander Temur. It is in this battle that famous poet Amir Khusrau was made captive by the Mongols.[60] Muhammad was succeeded by his son Kaikhusrau and after few months of this event Balban died.[61]

Kaiqubad was brought on the throne after Balban's death by the nobles of Delhi and Kaikhusrau continued at Multan till he fell to the conspiracy of Nizamuddin. Amir Khusrau in his *Qiranus Sadain* mentions that Tamar Khan again invaded the frontier and ravaged the territory between Lahore and Samana early in 686/1287, but retreated on the arrival of Malik Bektars with an imperial force from Delhi, they were routed up to the foothills of Jammu.[62] Due to the conspiracy, at the court many nobles were removed by Nizamuddin and responsibility of frontier fell on Jalaluddin Khalji who served as the *muqta* of Kaithal and *naib* of Samana during Balban's reign.[63] He later founded the Khalji dynasty in 1290.

So far, the Ilbari Turks or the Mamluk Sultans could not control the area beyond the river Beas, hence the whole Punjab, Sind and frontier region either remained under the Mongols or vassal rulers of the Mongols. The Khaljis were true imperialists and conquered almost whole of North India and sent expeditions into the South. But their relations with the Mongols were hardly friendly and there was not much progress in recovering the areas from their hands due to the harsh policy of the Chaghatais towards India.

Jalaluddin Khalji followed a comparatively policy of peace and failed to understand the importance of frontier defense. Peter Jackson refers two Mongol invasions one after the other in the years 690/1291 and 691/1292. The first one is based on the *Miftahul Futuh* of Amir Khusrau and the second of course mentioned by a number of contemporary chroniclers. The second, being a significant as it was headed by Abdullah son of Hulegu Khan. After some skirmishing between the two vanguards, however, a truce was declared. Jalaluddin and Abdullah exchanged friendly gifts and messages and the Mongol prince withdrew leaving behind a group of his followers under a commander named Alghu who accepted Islam. They got settled by the Sultan, in the neighborhood of Delhi. The Sultan gave one of his daughters in marriage to Alghu Khan.[64] It has been suggested the sultan seems to have been quite ignorant of the struggle that was going on amongst the descendant of Chinghiz Khan. As a result of this struggle quite a large number of Mongols had lost their homeland partly for this reason and many of them had decided to stay in India. Therefore, the situation remained same as it was under the Ilbari Turks.[65]

Alauddin Khalji ascended the throne of Delhi in 675/1296 after murdering Sultan Jalaluddin Khalji. He had to bear the brunt of the Mongol invasions for about a decade. The cause of these raids lay primarily in the political conditions prevailing in Central Asia. Dava, a descendant of Chaghatai in alliance with Qaidu, the descendant of Ogedei, started a struggle against the Ilkhans of Persia and the Great Khan in China. Kubalai Khan in China and the Ilkhans of Persia formed one group. Qaidu considered the Great Khan as usurper and made attempts to wrest the empire from him. Dava also had a special grudge against Kubalai Khan because of his interference in Transoxiana. Dava succeeded in Afghanistan. It was in the course of this struggle that Dava whenever pressed hard sent expeditions to India in search of resources both men and money. Besides, whenever, his men lost some ground, they managed to cross the Indian borders and even marched into the interior plains of northern India. It has been stated that Chinghiz and his immediate successors had been deterred from invading India by the heat of the plains, the house of Chaghatai was bolder; the Indus was repeatedly crossed. Multan and Lahore were more than once plundered.[66] It is thus in this background that Alauddin had to face the Mongol raids continuously.[67]

If we believe Ziauddin Barani, Alauddin Khalji was too ambitious who had conquered many territories and brought a lot of wealth. He began to dream of becoming Alexander. "God Almighty gave the blessed Prophet four friends, through where energy and power, the law and religion were established and through this establishment of law and religion, the name of the Prophet will endure to the Day of Judgement. God has given me also four friends, Ulugh Khan, Zafar Khan, Nusrat Khan and Alp Khan who through my prosperity, have attained to princely power and dignity. If I am so inclined, I can with the help of these four friends, establish a new religion and creed; and my sword, and the swords of my friends, will bring all men to adopt it. . . . I have wealth and elephants and forces beyond all calculations. My wish is to place Delhi in change of a vice regent and then I will go out myself into the world like Alexander in pursuit of conquest and subdue the whole habitable world."[68]

Alauddin took advice of Malik Alaulmulk, uncle of Barani in this regard who said, "My advice is that Your Majesty should never talk about these matters. Your Majesty knows what rivers of blood Chinghiz Khan made to flow in Muhammadan cities, but he never was able to establish the Mughal (Mongols) religion or institutions among Muhammadans. Many Mughals (Mongols) have turned Mussalmans but no Mussalman has ever become a Mughal."[69] Instead he advised the Sultan to make conquests in the country, to suppress the Mongols and repair the forts and appoint powerful officers in the frontier areas. Alauddin acted upon the advice of Alaulmulk and took to the task of conquering Hindustan and to push back the Mongols.[70]

On the basis of the contemporary works, the earliest evidence of operation in India by the Central Asian Mongols belongs to 697/1297-98, when Qaidu's *noyan* Kadar invaded the Panjab, ravaging the territory as far as the neighborhood of Qasur. But Ulugh Khan crushed the invaders at a locality Jaran Manjur near the banks of the Sutlej on 6 February 1298. The Mongol dead numbered 20,000 and the prisoners were taken to Delhi to be executed. A greater threat was posed by the forces of Qutlugh Khwaja. In *Jamiut Tawarikh* we are informed that Dua had sons, one of whom was Qutluq-Khawaja, to whom they have entrusted the province of Ghazni and the Qarauna army, which had long connections with them. In the summer they sat in the region of Ghur and Gharchistan and in the winter in the province of Ghazni and that area. They had constantly to do battle with Sultan of Delhi, and the army of Delhi had frequently defeated them. On every occasion they entered the borderlands of this country, robbing and plundering.[71] Their first major strike occurred in 699/1299-1300 during the absence of Delhi army on the first Gujrat campaign, with which Egyptian sources expressly link it. Qutlugh Khwaja, accompanied by his brother Temur Buqa, advanced directly on Delhi. Alauddin met the Mongols at Kili, some fifteen miles north of the capital. His right wing, led by Zafar Khan, crushed the Mongol left, but on the way back from the pursuit was ambushed by the enemy rearguard under the *noyan* Targhi and annihilated. Yet the Mongol army then retired. The reason of their retiring has been given that Qutlugh Khwaja was mortally wounded who died on the way.[72]

Over the next few years, Mongol bands number 10000 or 15000 continued to make plundering raids on the Panjab but caused no general harm and retired on each occasion without a pitched battle. But when in 702/1302-03, Alauddin's forces were again scattered on distant campaigns, Targhi now in command of the Mongol armies, felt strong enough to threaten Delhi a second time. Alauddin was reduced to following the defensive tactics he had eschewed during the earlier attack, barricading himself and his army in the Siri plain. The Mongols' position extended from the Yamuna as far as the plain of Lohrawat; but although they launched raids into the suburbs of the old city, where they penetrated as far as the *Hauz-i-khas,* they were unable to move there in force for fear of exposing their flank. This stalement situation lasted for two months; then Targhi suddenly withdrew to his own territory.[73]

Targhi's retreat was widely regarded as one of the miracle of the age and certainly the sources offer no explanation. More probably, his attention was demanded by events beyond the Oxus. However, his invasion roused Alauddin Khalji to repair various fortresses lying on the path of the Mongol advance, Kaithal was refortified, and an inscription on the Barsi Gate at Hansi enables us to date the restoration here in November 1303. The Sultan also enacted various fiscal and administrative measures, designed to increase the armed forces and to avert any repetition of the crisis. The *iqtas* on the routes of Mongols were placed under experienced nobles and whole route was secured by the appointment of tried and vigilant generals.[74]

Before these measures could take shape the Mongols in AD 703/1304 under the leadership of Ali Beg and Tartaq proceeded along the foot of Sirmur hills to the bank of the Beas and while a portion of their army harried Nagore, the main army marched to Doab, between the Ganges and the Jumna. This was soon checked jointly checked by Malik Kafur and Ghazi Malik who captured large numbers of them.[75] The Mongol next appeared under the leadership of Kank or Gung and invaded region of Khekar on the river Ghaggar. Malik Kafur and Ghazi were again sent against them. Their leader Kank was made captive and sent to Delhi.[76]

By now the measures taken by Alauddin Khalji must have taken shape. Ghazi Malik was appointed as the warden of the marches with his headquarters at Dipalpur, where he remained till the death of Alauddin. Once again the Mongols appeared under their leader Iqbal Mandah but were defeated and made captives. It is believed that Ghazi Malik now adopted an offensive policy and made attacks on Ghazni. By this time they had ceased to invade India. But it does not appear whether the Sultnate had a control beyond Ravi. Ghazi Malik is said to have got Alauddin's *khutba* read in Ghazmi. But this statement, has been challenged by the scholars.[77] Barani highly speaks of Ghazi Malik who took every year an expedition in winter in Mongols' territories and had become the 'Wall of China' against them.[78] Ibn Battuta saw an inscription in the mosque at Multan in which Tughluq himself laid claim to twenty-nine victories over the Mongols alone.[79]

There is a reference of an embassy from Iran through which Oljaitu demanded Alauddin's submission and the hand of a Khalji princess in marriage. But it did not bear any fruit, since the envoys were detained and eighteen members of their suite were crushed beneath the feet of elephants.[80]

Barani asserts that due to the measures taken by Alauddin, there was a respite from the Mongols' attacks until the end of the reign of Qutubuddin Mubarkshah (720/1320) . Amir Khusrau claims that Qutubuddin contemplated the conquest of Ghazni but was dissuaded by his *amirs.* However, we find reference of a Mongol invasion in the year 721/1321 which was made unsuccessful by the Delhi forces who brought the Mongols along with their leader as prisoners.[81] The last Mongol invasion has been mentioned during the reign of Muhammad bin Tughluq when Tarmashirin entered the frontier. Later, the sources speak of the exchanging of embassies between Delhi and Iran and good relations also prevailed between Muhammad bin Tughluq and Tarmashirin and thus incursions on India ceased till the invasion of Timur in 1398.[82]

In the end one has to seek an enquiry into the causes, which did not allow the Mongols to penetrate into the Indian plains on permanent basis. No doubt they tried their luck and many time succeeded to control the vast area in the northwest frontier region of the sultanate either by appointing their own *nuyin* or a *shahna* or accepted the ruling amirs as their tributary. As far direct control is concerned the Mongol hardly established their administration in these areas where the *Yasa* of Chinghiz could prevail. The dream of Chinghiz to conquer the world by his successors remained unfulfilled though most of the known half world was in their jurisdiction. K.S. Lal in his *History of the Khaljis* was first among the Indian scholars who logically put forwards certain causes for the failure of the Mongols in India under the title *causes of the defeat of the Mongols* obviously during the period of

Alauddin Khalji as under:

"Before closing this chapter 'The Mongol Invasion' it would be interesting to study why the Mughals, who once terrorized both the east and the west and who even in the time of Alauddin waged mighty wars in Central Asia, were always successfully defeated by the armies of Hindustan. The defeats and retreats of the Mughals in India were due to many reasons.

Firstly, the idea of world conquest, which had been the driving force of the Mughal empire, was given up on account of the wars among the various descendants of Chinghiz Khan. The Mughals who invaded India, were sent by the Khans of Transoxiana. They had rebelled against the Great Khans of China and were mostly busy with their internal troubles in Cental Asia. Dava Khan, the arch enemy of Hindustan fought some forty battles in Central Asia itself and consequently could not give all his attention and energy to the conquerst of Hindustan. As Professor Habib rightly points out, the discord among the Mughals and their own inter-cine warfare saved the kingdom of Delhi which could not have withstood a united attack of the Mughals".

"Secondly, the numbers that invaded India seem to be exaggerated. Women, children and old men-all accompanied the invaders and although as such the number of the invaders was inflated, their military efficiency was marred. On many occasions Alauddin took prisoner a large number of women and children and sold them in the market of Delhi or put them to the sword."

Thirdly, the qualities of the early Mongols, which had given them magnificent success in the early days of their history, were now extinct. The agility, the mobility and the qualities of patience and endurance no longer marked the Mongols who invaded India, and it is strange indeed that on an occasion of the two sieges of Delhi in 1300 and 1303, Alauddin exhausted the patience of the Mughals and they retired without giving tough fights such as were needed for the conquest of an empire".

"Fourthly, Dawa Khan, who ruled for thirty two years, could send organized expeditions to India in spite of his engagement in Central Asia. His death in 1306 brought about disorder in Transoxiana, within a period of two or three years three Khans—Kuyuk, Kubak and Taliku, ascended the throne. Even after that the affairs were not set right and Kubak had to abdicate. He was reinstated in 1321. In these circumstances Mughal invasions to India could not be organized and sent at regular intervals. On the contrary Ghazi Tughlaq used to harass the Mughals themselves".

"And lastly, the main cause of the Mughal defeat lies in the fact that they had come to fight with a king who himself was a war-lord. The patience, integrity and the military genius of Alauddin as well as his courage and perseverance are already manifested in his talk with Malik Alaulmulk who tried to dissuade him from fighting Qutlugh Khwaja—Alauddin thought it his bounded duty to fight the foreign foe. He effected various reforms, he raised a huge army and through studied determination always repulsed the Mughal inroads until they stopped altogether."[83]

Peter Jackson has brought his thesis that in the frontier region as well as in Afghanistan during this period there was an advent of the Negudaris or Qaraunas who more or less controlled the area and were allying themselves with the Mongols. According to him the Indian sources never refer to Nagudaris, but they do occasionally employ the term Qaraunah.[84]

Under the sub-title 'Plunder or conquest' Jackson on the basis of Wassaf, Badaoni and versions of others suggests that the aim of the Mongols on an occasion was actually to conquer the sultanate.[85] But in the conclusion he suggests that the real aim of the Mongols was to procure slaves from India and in support he quotes the campaign of Sali Noyan's in Kashmir and India when he yielded Hulegu Khan a great booty of Indian slaves, according to Rashiduddin Fazlullah, the descendants of these slaves were still found on the royal estates in Persia. Jackson further gives an example of Amir Khusrau who was also made captive by the Mongols. The second aim could be to plunder items of booty especially horses from the Khokhars' territory that produced choice mounts. We can also presumably take it for granted that the Mongols came in the hope of acquiring gold and silver and in this connection we may have an explanation for India's enhanced attractiveness. With the ambitious raids on independent Hindu kingdoms in the south from 695/1296 onwards, Delhi's rulers were known to be amassing great quantities of spices, of which the Mongols, consequently, must have been tempted to relieve them.[86] One may add to this statement the remarks of E.D. Phillips who let us believe that Qubilai Khan demanded tribute from various rulers in southern India and Ceylon, who formally acknowledged him as suzerain, no doubt with some hope of advantage.[87] The sultanate proved too powerful to be conquered, hence only raids and raids, which were occasional and destructive but transitory.

References

1. *Tabakat-i-Nasiri*, pp. 270-72.
2. Ibid., p. 272. For more details, see *Turkestan Down to the Mongol Invasion*, pp. 393-96 and *History of the World Conqueror*, pp. 77-79.
3. *Tabakat-I-Nasiri*, pp. 273-74.
4. Ibid., pp. 274-79. Also see Howorth, *History of the Mongols*, I, I,I pp. 83-84 and *Comprehensive History of India*, v, pp. 67-68.
5. *Tabakat-i-Nasiri*, pp. 288-99.
6. *History of the World Conqueror*, pp. 133-35 and *Turkestan Down to the Mongol Invasion*, pp. 445-46. See, J. Curtin, *The Mongols: A History* (Boston, 1908), p. 128.
7. See Geoge Vernodsky, *The Mongols and Russia* (Yale, 1953) , pp. 40-41.
8. Ibid., p. 139.
9. *Tabakat-i-Nasiri*, p. 1082-84.
10. *The History and the Life of Chinggis Khan* (*The Secretet History of the Mongols*) trams. and annotated Urgunge Onon (E.J. Brill, 1990), pp. 155-56.
11. *History of the World Conqueror*, pp. 141-42.

12. Ibid., pp. 143-47.
13. Ibid., pp. 459-60.
14. *Tabakat-i-Nasiri,* pp. 609-10.
15. The chief's name was Rai Kakar Sankin 'Raja of the Khokars'. See *History of the World Conqueror,* pp. 413-14 and 9n. Also see Elliot Dowson, ii, pp. 237, 396 and 396n.
16. *Tabakat-i-Nasiri,* pp. 1045-46. A modern scholar doubts whether the Delhi Sultan could effectively stop the Mongols if he had decided to march through despite of his reported refusal. That Chinghiz yet respected Delhi's sovereignty and in the winter of 1222, marched back through the Hindukush, speaks well of his moderation and his scrupulous observance of international practice. A.B.M. Habibullah, *The Foundation of Muslim Rule in India* (Allahabad 1961), p. 206.
17. *Tabakat-i-Nasiri,* 1043-46 , 1n.
18. *Al-Hind,* ii, pp. 202-3.
19. Weatherford Jack, *Genghis Khan and the Making of Modern World* (New York, 2004) , p. 126.
20. *History of the World Conqueror,* pp. 411-13.
21. ibid, p. 142.
22. Ibid., pp. 414-59.
23. Minhaj, p. 179; Aloo see I.H. Siddiqui; 'The Qarlugh Kingdom in the North-Western India During the Thirteenth Century' published in *Islamic Culture,* vol. LIV No. 2, April 1980, pp. 75-90. Nangrahar has been described by Babur in his Tuzuk, as one of the Sub-divisions of Kabul country. He writes, "It grows good crops of rice and corn, excellent and abundant oranges, citrons and pomegranates" See *Baburnama,* pp. 207-8. Also see G.D. Gulati, *India's Northwest Frontier,* pp. 24-25.
24. *The Successors of Genghis Khan,* p. 55 and *Tabakat-I-Nasiri,* p. 1126, 6n. Also I.H. Siddiqui, 'The Qarlugh Kingdom in the North-Western India during the Thirteenth Century,' op.cit.
25. I.H. Siddiqui, 'Qarlugh Kingdom,' op. cit.
26. Edward Thomas, *The Chronicles of the Pathan Kings of Delhi* (Delhi, 1967), pp. 92-96.
27. G.D. Gulati, *India's North West Frontier,* p. 26.
28. *Tabakat-i-Nasiri,* pp. 1132-33.
29. ibid; pp. 1133-36.
30. For the role of the Khokhans see G.D. Gulati, *India's North West Frontier,* pp. 49-58.
31. Minhaj (p. 270) in *Audi Turk Kalin Bharat,* p. 75 and G.D. Gulati, op. cit., p. 28.
32. 'Qarlugh Kingdom,' p. 81.
33. Ibid., p. 83-86.
34. *Tabakat-i-Nasiri,* pp. 537-39. At another place Minhaj gives a

contradictory statement and mentions that Turti had left Chinghiz Khan and joined Jalaluddin Mangbarni and became a convert to the Muhammadan faith. It needs to be clarified see *Tabakat-i-Nasiri,* p. 297.

35. *Al-Hind,* ii, p. 203.
36. *Tabakat-I-Nasiri,* p. 1293.
37. Ibid., p. 539.
38. Ibid., p. 541.
39. Ibid., p. 544.
40. Peter Jackson, *The Delhi Sultanate,* p. 105.
41. 'Qarlugh Kingdom' pp. 75-90.
42. A.B.M. Habibullah, *Foundatios of Muslim Rule in India,* op. cit. pp. 210-12 and Peter Jackson, op.cit., p. 105.
43. For more details see G.D. Gulati 'Lahore during thirteenth and fourteenth centuries' published in the *Proceedings of Panjab History Conference* (Patiala,1980) ; Joginder K. Chawla, 'Sack of Lahore in 1241 and its impact on the trading activities' published in the *Proceedings of Panjab History Conference*[Patiala,1997) ; *Tabakat-i-Nasiri,* pp. 1133-36, 1142; *Comprehensive History of India,* v, p. 246; *Foundation of Muslim Rule in India,* p. 212 and Peter Jackson, op.cit. p. 105.
44. *Tabakat-i-Nasiri,* pp. 815 and 1153-55.
45. *Comprehensive History of India,* v, p. 255.
46. This is based on the *Tarikh Nama-i-Herat* of Saifi Haravi ed. M.Z. Siddiqui, Calcutta, 1944, pp. 156-57 and quoted in *Foundation of Muslim Rule in India,* p. 214 and p. 228 note 49. Minhaj has been charged with concealing this event, see *Tabakat-i-Nasiri,* p. 1201n.
47. *Foundation of Muslim Rule in India,* p.214.
48. ibid, pp. 214-15.
49. See G.D. Gulati, "Role of the governors in the North-west frontier" in the *Proceedings of the Indian History Congress* (Bombay.1980) , pp.
50. *Tabakat-I-Nasiri,* p. 277 and *Foundation of Muslim Rule in India,* op.cit, p. 215.
51. *Foundation of Muslim Rule in India,,* op.cit., p. 215. At one place Minhaj mentions that Lahore had become the fief of Jalaluddin Masud Shah. It was still in ruins and was not rebuilt until some time later. According to Raverty some authors state that Jalaluddin Masud Shah held Lahore independent of Delhi Kingdom, and was countenanced by the Mongols. See *Tabakati-i-Nasiri,* p. 700 and 8n.
52. *Tabakat-i-Nasiri,* pp. 677-79 and 814-15.
53. Ibid, pp.689 and 690, 8n.
54. Peter Jackson, op. cit, p. 111 U.N. Day, *Some Aspects of Medieval Indian History* (Delhi, 1971) , pp.39-40 and *Foundation of Muslim Rule in India,* pp. 215-19.
55. Ziauddin Barani, *Tarikh-i-Fizoze-Shahi,* Hindi Tr. S.A.A. Rizvi in *Aadi*

Turk Kalin Bharat (Aligarh, 1956) , pp. 159-60. Also see *Comprehensive History of India,* v, p. 280 and Elliot and Dowson, iii, pp. 102-3.

56. Ibid., p. U.N. Day op.cit., p. 41 and G.D. Gulati 'The Tribes in the North-west frontier Thirteenth and Fourteenth Centuries' published in *Proceedings of the Punjab History Conference* (Patiala,1979) .
57. Barani, op.cit. p.170. U.N. Day op.cit., p. 41.
58. Barani states "Often in those days the Mongol horsemen used to cross the Beas and enter the territory (of Delhi) . Balban used to dispatch Bughra Khan from Samana, Khan-i-Shahid (prince Muhammad) from Multan and Malik Bektars from Delhi (to fight them) . They would then march up to the river Beas and expel the Mongols. In this manner they obtained several victories and as a result, the Mongols never dared approach the river any more". See Barani, op. cit. p. 180. See also U.N. Day, op.cit.pp.42-43 and A.B.M. Habibullah, op.cit.p.223. Also *Comprehensive History of India,* v, pp.297-99.
59. Isami, *Futuh-us-Salatin,* Eng. Tr. Mahdi Hussain, pp.299-300. Also Peter ackson, op.cit., p. 117.
60. Ferishta, *Rise of the Mahomden Power in Hindustan,*I, p.143 and Peter Jackson, op.cit., p. 117. However, Amir Khusrau managed to escape. See U.N. Day, op.ci., p. 44.
61. Barani, op.cit., p. 201.
62. Peter Jackson, p. 118 and U.N. Day p. 44. Yahya Bin Ahmad Sirhindi refers one Khan-i-Jahan Shahik Barbak as the leader of the imperial army. See *Tarikh-i-Mubarakshahi,* Eng. trans. (Baroda), p. 51.
63. Peter Jackson, p. 118 and *Comprehensive History of India,* v, p. 308.
64. Barani mentions that the climate of Delhi and its neighborhood did not suit to them hence they returned back to their country. See *Tarikh-i-Firozeshahi,* pp. 218-219 in *Khalji Kalin Bharat,* pp. 27-28. Peter ackson op.cit., p. 118; U.N. Day, op. cit., pp.46-47 and *Comprehensive History of India,* v, p. 317.
65. U.N. Day, op.cit, p. 48.
66. Saunders, J.J., *The History of the Mongol Conquests* (London, 1971), p. 172.
67. U.N. Day op. cit., pp.48-49, *Comprehensive History of India,* v, pp. 97-98. Peter Jackson devotes a full chapter on the Chaghtai invasions in which he has given detailed account of the Central Asian politics. See *Delhi Sultanate,* pp.217-20. According to K.S. Lal, Dava Khan of Trasoxiana, who was mostly unsuccessful against his adversaries, wanted to try his luck in India as well and constantly sent out expeditions to this country. He was a determined enemy of Hindustan and successfully snatched Ghazni from the Ilkhans and made it a base of his operations against India. See *History of the Khaljis,* pp. 151-52.
68. *Khalji Kalin Bharat,* p. 54.
69. Ibid., pp. 55-56.

70. Ibid., pp. 58-59.
71. Peter Jackson, op.cit., pp. 221-22.
72. Ibid., p. 222 and U.N. Day, p. 52.
73. Ibid., pp.223-24 and U.N. Day, pp. 52-53.
74. U.N. Day, op.cit., p. 53.
75. Ibid., p. 53 and Peter Jackson, pp. 227-28.
76. U.N. Day, p. 55-56.
77. K.S. Lal, (pp.175-76) gives the text of a letter written by Amir Khusrau in which it has been mentioned the *khutba* was read in a mosque of Ghazni.
78. Barani p. 322 in *Khalji Kalin Bharat,* p. 89.
79. H.A.R. Gibb, p. 649.
80. For full details of this embassy see Peter Jackson, p. 225 and note 57.
81. Peter Jackson, p. 231.
82. Ibid, pp. 232-35.
83. K.S. Lal, *History of the Khalis,* pp.177-79.
84. *Delhi Sultanate,* pp.115-16 and Appendix III, p. 328.
85. Ibid., p. 235. Badauni states, "A second time Qutlugh Khwaja, the son of Dua, came from Mawarnnahr with a countless host to attempt the conquest of Hindustan and penetrated as far as Delhi, inflicting no injury on the districts through which he passed." Zafar Khan and Ulugh Khan defeated them. Qutlugh Khwaja made his way to Khurasan where he died. See *Muntakhabu-t-Tawarikh,* Eng. trans. S.A., Ranking, I, pp. 249-50.
86. *Delhi Sultanate,* pp. 235-37.
87. E.D. Philips, The Mongols (London, 1969), p. 109.

6

Commercial Networks

PHYSICAL FEATURES MADE Central Asia, the land of steppes and pastures famous for breeding of horses. The region had trade dominions of the best portions of the earth passing through which the silk route made the country commercially important. It can rightly be termed as the *Heart of Asia.*[1] The region had played a significant role bringing together the two continents i.e. Asia and Europe. The so-called "silk route" was in operation by the century before Christ and that it reached on early peak during the period from 50-150 A.D., when the Roman, Parthian, Kushan, and Han empires dominated the political landscape of Eurasia.[2] And the continued commercial relations among different countries reached its height during thirteenth century with the advent of the Chinggisds and the creation of their vast and unprecedented transcontinental empire. It could be possible because of the assured and definite role played by the contemporary rulers viz. the Mongols in Central Asia, Iran, Golden Horde and China; Turks in India; Mamluks in Syria and Christian power in Europe. Basically it was the common interest of all the ruling dynasties: the investment in improving trade routes, maintaining a favourable trans-regional commercial climate, as well as their patronage of different merchant communities. This period was the period of adventurers and explorers, who not only fulfilled their own ambitions but also opened the new vistas for the trading communities as well as missionaries. Therefore, it is pertinent to seek an enquiry into the motives and missions of the medieval travellers and the attitude of the ruling class. It will make us to understand the commercial networks going under changes.

Needless to state that the Mongols had become the most powerful political entity and they had monopolized over the trade routes through Central Asia, Iran, Kipchak and China. In the contemporary literature, we find enough evidence regarding an explicit and favourable attitude of the Mongols towards trade and commerce. The traders had to seek their permission before entering into their vast empire. On the other hand, it was the duty of the Mongols to provide them the safe conduct and protection on their journeys with goods and caravans. Not only promoters of trade and commerce, "the Mongols, themselves were experienced traders by the time of their conquests" as stated in a recent article on 'Steppe' in the *The New Encyclopedia Britannica* in its twenty-eighth volume. It further reads "Caravans, moved freely throughout their domains and thousands, perhaps tens of thousands, of persons traveled between Europe and China. Marco Polo's account of his remarkable career in the service of Kubilai Khan in China shows how readily the Mongols employed strangers and welcomed merchants from distant lands. Chinese silks were then superior to those of other parts of the world. Consequently, intensified communi-cations under the Mongols allowed the diffusion of certain Chinese skills and tastes to the rest of Eurasia. Gunpowder, the compass and printing were especially important for Europe. In the Middle East, it was Chinese luxuries such as silk, porcelain and styles of painting that had the most obvious impact.[3]

Before the rise of the Mongols, there had already developed an elaborate system of roads radiating from

Baghdad to serve not only the movements of armies but also of caravans of merchants.[4] The Khurasan road system and other high roads were in progress under the Abbasids, which intersected various parts of Central Asia and Persia, had on its edges several facilities. Security on the roads had become a common feature of that period. Insfandiyar informs us that the taxes on the imports of Tabaristan were light especially under the rule of the Buwands.[5] The Khwarizmians were ambitious travellers and their merchants traveled across the Eurasion steppes as far as Southern Russia and even the Danube basin where certain place names attest their presence. Yakut, a vast travelled geographer (*d.* AD 1229) writing on the eve of the Mongol invasions mentions that he had never seen such prosperity in urban and agricultural fields as in Khwarizm.[6]

The Mongols had a typical pastoral economy before establishing a strong unified well- organized empire. To the people of the steppes with limited resources, trade was of vital importance, their basic product, the horses had to be bartered for agricultural products and other goods, as has been described by Juwaini. He writes, "They were not settled in any town and there was no concourse of merchants and travelers to them, articles of dress were a great rarity among them and advantages of trading with them well-known."[7]

Chinghiz Khan had organized a postal service on the grand routes to facilitate the travellers, the couriers and public officers on their journeys. The Horses, carriages, and food were supplied by the inhabitants and the safety on the roads was provided by strict police regulations. H.H. Howorth in his monumental work *History of the Mongols* has rightly observed that for the first time probably in the history of Asia, it was possible to travel with perfect safety across the steppes of Turkistan[8] and rightly expressed that the history of the Mongols was not necessarily "a history of drum and trumpet."[9]

Chinghiz Khan showed genuine interest in travellers and

merchants. He used to receive them always with great warmth and zeal extending favours to them. The great Khan arranged the posting of *qaraqchis* (guards) on the highways and issued a *yasa* (a mandatory injection) that whenever a merchant arrived in his territory, should be granted a safe conduct and the merchandise if worthy of Khan's acceptance should be sent directly to him along with the owner. Those days, the Mongols always treated the Muslim merchants with respect and for their dignity would erect for them clean tents of white tents.[10] They were permitted to use *yam* (post-horses) facilities free of charges. Mares and sheep were to be kept at each station to supply *kumis* (a kind of beverage) and meat to the travellers.[11]

Promotion of trade with the outer, world was on his agenda. First of all he looked forward to his immediate neighbourer Khwarzm Shah of Khwarizm. A commercial treaty was drafted in the year 1218 A.D. between the two. Chinghiz Khan sent a caravan of five hundred merchants, all Muslims, with gold, silver, silk and sable, etc. for Khwarizm, with the message, "I am the sovereign of the sunset. Let there be between us a firm treaty of friendship, amity and peace, and let traders and *karawans* on both sides come and go, and let the precious products and ordinary commodities which may be in my territory be conveyed by them into thine and those of thine, in the same manner, let them bring into mine."[12] However, they were killed on their way to Otrar, a border town of Khwarizm. Their goods were seized by the governor of the city with the exception of a camel man who carried this terrible news to Chinghiz Khan. This act of barbarity was contrary to Chinghiz Khan's policy of protecting the commercial classes. This led to a war between the Mongols and Khwarizm Shah.[13] Chinghiz Khan called Khwarizm Shah, *aghzi*, signifying a robber.[14]

The countries of Ajam, Iran, Khwarizm and Ghazni had become one trade unit and one Khwaja Shamsuddin Ajami was the *malik-ut-tujjar,* 'chief of the merchants' of this unit.

He visited the court of Sultan Iluttmish in Delhi.[15] New routes were discovered during course of Mongol invasions and it was the duty of the rulers to safeguard the trade routes, so that the caravans of merchants could move unmolested and uninterrupted. Minhaj, the author of *Tabakat-i-Nasiri,* was sent twice for the adjustment of trade routes disturbed during the Mongol incursions.[16]

The policy of protecting the traders and trade routes continued under the successors of Chinghiz Khan. Ogedei Khan was with the fairest of dispositions and the noblest of qualities and customs. He was always exercising the utmost generosity and liberality towards all the classes of people. The love of justice and bounty had gained such mastery over his nature that not for the twinkling of an eye would he neglect the spreading the equity and the diffusion of beneficence. Sometimes the pillars of state and the great men of the Court would object to his excessive generosity and he would say: "It is known of a certainty to all mankind that the world is faithful to none and that wisdom requires a man to keep himself alive by the perpetuation of a good name."[17] He got the city of Karakorum built on the bank of river Orkhon. In addition to *tayan yam,* other *yams* were also established. For the protection of the *yam, a tuman* was posted at every stage. A *yasa* was issued that every day five wagons fully loaded with food and drink should arrive from the provinces to be placed in stores and then dispensed there from. For corn and wine there were provided great wagon drawn by six oxen each.[18] All the historical sources, even those absolutely independent of the Mongol Khans and hostile to them, extol the magnanimity and leniency of Ogodei Khan.[19] The Mongol epic *Secret History of the Mongols* attributes the following words to the great Khan, "Our king Chinghiz created to royal house at the court of great labour. Now is the time to bring peace and plenty to the peoples and not to lay burdens upon them."[20]

Ogedei Khan (AD 1228-41) was a great friend of the

Muslims and his favours to the people, engaged in trade was an example. When a person reached to him for money so that he could begin trade, the attendants told that he was already in debt. Ogodei ordered that he be given double of the amount he asked for, so that he must pay his debts and then begins the trade.[21] As is known there had been no agriculture in the neighbourhood of Karakorum on account of excessive cold, but a beginning was made during Ogodei time. A certain person planted radishes and a few of them grew. He brought them to Qa'an, who ordered them to be counted with their leaves. The number came to a hundred, and he ordered the man to be given 100 *balish*.[22]

When the fame of his bounty and beneficence had been spread throughout the world, merchants made their way to his court from every side. He would command their wares to be bought, whether they were good or bad, and full price paid. Some people from India brought him two tusks of ivory. He asked what they wanted and was told "500 *balish*". With out the slightest hesitation he ordered them to be given this amount. The officers of the court made a great outcry, asking how he could give so large a sum for so contemptible a matter, where these people had come from an enemy country "No one", he replied, "is an enemy of mine. Give them the money and let them go."[23]

Persian chroniclers held in high esteem Mongke Khan whose honesty and generosity had always attracted traders. They were paid against the deal done in the reign of his predecessor Guyuk Khan. Ata Malik Juvaini and Rashiduddin Fazlullah both narrate an anecdote in which they give a detailed account of some merchants who had delivered their wares but the price had not yet been fixed and others had not yet received a draft or money and money had not yet reached the stage of a transfer that Guyuk Khan died. When Mongke Khan succeeded the throne three merchants approached him in the hope of receiving their dues against their transactions. The officials at the court felt there was no obligation to pay the amount due on these transactions out of the Khan's treasury. The payment could be refused but Mangu Khan out of his generosity and favours gave orders for the full payment to the merchants which amounted to more than 5,00,000 silver balish. "And from what book of history has it been read or heard from reciters", writes Juwaini, "that a King paid the debt of another King."[24]

Marco Polo writing about Cambluc (Beijing), capital of Qubilai Khan, informs us that it had numerous hostelries for the merchants coming from different countries. His account makes a special mention about the roads and highways connecting with each other. He described about the *Yamb* (Horse-Post House) and paper-currency called *chao* which played a significant role in the economy of China.[25] About the cities of Persia he writes, "There are traders and artisans who live by their labour and crafts weaving cloths of gold and silk stuff of sundry kinds. They have plenty of cotton produced in the country and abundance of wheat, barley, millet and wine, with fruits of all kinds."[26]

Under the Ilkhans Persia witnessed the revival of its economy. Halaku after the sack of Baghdad and the conquest of Persia immediately took to the task of restoration in those kingdoms. The creator of the Ilkhanate of Persia (1256-1349 A.D.) appointed a number of Muslim administrators including the medieval chronicler Ata Malik Juvaini to devote themselves to the cause of peace and prosperity. They became reputed protectors of merchants and artisans. The traders were encouraged to trade in his kingdom and for this he readily paid exorbitantly for the goods brought by them.[27] V.V. Barthold suggests that throughout that period and despite the complaints of contemporaries about the utter ruin of the country and the complete decadence of learning, Persia held first place in the contemporary world, culturally and in all probability economically also. Taste for urban life was felt steadily and new centers of trade sprang up which continued to be important even after the Mongol onslaught.

Destruction of the caliphate made it easier for the followers of other creeds to take part in intellectual life together with the Muslims. The Mongol monarchs patronized secular science.[28]

Ghazan Khan, who is known as the greatest of the Ilkhans, was a versatile figure. He was well versed with arts and science such as natural history, medicine, astronomy and chemistry, and also in the art of goldsmith, blacksmith, carpenter, painter, founder or turner more efficiently than the master of these trades. No one could surpass him in making saddles, bridles, spurs, greaves and helmets. He could hammer, stitch and polish and usually spent his leisure hours in such occupations.[29] Ghazan Khan earned fame by introducing number of reforms and abolishing many taxes in order to encourage the merchants and their caravans. Many foreign merchants used to make frequent visits to his kingdom.[30] He also introduced one single system of weight and measure throughout the kingdom.[31] This policy of reforms continued under his brother and successor Oljaitu. For the convenience of the traders and travelers he got his entire kingdom surveyed in 1311 A.D. for the erection of milestones. Sultaniya, built during his regime, soon became the center of multifarious activities, which was connected with roads from all sides.[32] Abu Sa'id continued the same policy of extending facilities to the traders in addition to abolishing several taxes. He issued a diploma allowing the Venetian traders free ingress to Persia and to stay where they liked, and to be allowed to feed their horses for three days at the post stations.[33]

The eastern countries from the beginning of the Fifth Clime on the bank of the Oxus to the farthest limits of Khitai, which are the First Clime, according to Juvaini were placed under Mahmud Yalvach and his worthy son Masud Beg. Under their governorship Central Asia recovered soon from the ruinous conditions. Bukhara had already attained its property under these wealthy merchants.[34]

Barka Khan, the ruler of Kipchak (Golden Horde) embraced Islam which paved the way to the process for the Muslim merchants to traverse his kingdom. The caravans made their way into various parts of the Horde and brought the Volga whatever China and Western Asia could offer. Serai had developed into a splendid city full of palaces and mosques. It became the leading center of Muslim civilization. From the south, Italian merchants traveled to the Golden Horde, which had opened several parts to them in Crimea.[35]

Thus throughout the Asian kingdoms peace and security was guaranteed. The Mongol rulers exemplified their kingship at its best by providing effective administration and protection for the merchant community. Once their conquests had united under a single suzerainty the Chinese and Middle Eastern centers of civilization and the regions between, overland trade along well-maintained and policed routes flourished as never before or since.[36] And it was due to these favourable conditions prevailing in the domains of the Mongol Khans that Marco Polo, Ibn Battuta and other medieval travellers could undertake their journeys through these lands. The missionaries of Plano Carpini, Rubruck and others also traveled from Rome to the Far East. It has been maintained that the silk-route of antiquity, which criss-crossed the regions enabling a reciprocal east-west, north-south traffic of goods was revived under the Mongols.[37] Therefore, the general impression that the Mongol conquests were nothing but surge of chaotic elemental savages who crushed everything by the weight of their numbers and destroyed the culture they could not understand seems incorrect.[38]

For almost a century from about 1240 to about 1340, the unprecedented unification of much Central Asia under the Mongol empire permitted safe travel between China and Western Europe for the first time in the history. The Mongols by way of opening China to the west also brought the Near East to their contact, which had already close contact with South Asia by sea. Hence the whole commercial network included the various regions of Asia and Europe through land or sea thus joining the whole Islamic world and Christian world together under the economic needs of the period. We find a reference of traders having their business running successfully in a number of towns in various directions. For example, the Arab geographer Yaqut al-Rumi (1179-1229) observed that a contemporary merchant maintained warehouses in Gujrat, Khwarizm, and Bulghar on the Volga. He was involved in the spice trade.[39]

The earliest definition of commerce we find in *Muqadimmah* in which Ibn Khaldun explains commerce as the art of increasing one's fortune by buying goods and selling them again at an increased price, either by storing them or awaiting an increase in price, or by taking them into another country where the price is higher.[40] Hence it required traveling and traversing the different regions in search of good profits. Long distance trade, as we know, had hardly been carried out by a single individual or a small group of people, as it involved a great risk during long journeys. There was always a risk of wild beasts, of plundering their goods by tribes and bandits, snow and desert and scarcity of water on the way. Therefore, to ensure safety of their lives and goods it was advisable to travel in caravans.[41]

Merchants usually attached themselves to pilgrim caravans because they were more secure though some pilgrims invariably perished along the way every year from exposure, thirst, flash food, epidemic, or even attack by local nomads. In 1361 A.D., 100 Syrian pilgrims died of extreme winter cold; in 1430 A.D., 3000 Egyptian perished of heat and thirst.[42] Even in the nineteenth century when Alexander Burnes took is travels into Bukhara he found deserts of Central Asia very risky. At a place he writes, "we had before heard of the deserts south of the Oxus; and had now the means of forming a judgement from personal observation. We saw the skeletons of camels and horses now bleaching in the sun, which had perished from thirst. The nature of the roads or pathways admits of their easy obliteration; and, if the beaten track be once forsaken, the traveler and his jaded animal generally perish. A circumstance of this very nature occurred a few days previous to our leaving Charjooee. A party of three persons traveling from the Orgunje camp lost the road, and their supply of water failed them. Two of their horses sank under the parching thirst; and the unfortunate men opened the vein of their surviving camel, sucked its blood and reached Charjooee from the nourishment, that they thus derived. The camel died. These are facts of frequent occurrence. The Khan of Orgunje, in his late march into the desert, lost upwards of two thousand camels, that had been loaded with water and provisions for his men." [43]

Caravan, a word of Persian origin, signifies a group of merchants, pilgrims or travelers, journeying together usually for mutual protection. In the deserts of Asia and north Africa the animals mostly used was the camel, because of its catholic appetite, its hardiness and its loading capacity. In hot weather, on a long journey, a camel ordinarily carried about 350 pounds, but on shorter journeys, in cooler weather, or to evade custom duties the load might be increased to 1000 pound. The camels were supplied by the merchants or travelers or hired from neighbouring nomads, Arabs, Kazakhs or Mongols, who were often also the drivers, being not only skilled camel herdsmen, familiar with the routes, but also by their presence conferring some protection from other nomads. The leader of the caravan, elected by the members, was frequently a nomad chief. He decided the order of march and stopping places. The size of the caravan was dependent upon the amount of traffic, the insecurity of the route, and the availability of camels. The largest recorded caravans were those for special purposes, e.g., the pilgrim caravan from Cairo and Damascus to Mecca, which might include over 10,000 camels. The timing of caravans was governed by the availability of water and pasture or, in the case of the pilgrim caravans, by the need to be in Mecca on the 8th day of the month of Zar'l hijja. Consequently the Orenburg caravan left Bukhara after the melting of the winter snow, and the Basra caravan left Aleppo after the rains of late autumn. These times might have been modified by commercial considerations. The speed of a caravan varied with the heat, load, size and availability of water and pasture.[44]

Both Ibn Jubayr and Ibn Battuta left panoramic views of the Iraqi caravan after their departure from Mecca for Medina. Ibn Jubayr's description is as follows:

> "This assemblage of people of Iraq, Khurasan and Mossul, as well as those of other countries who have joined them to accompany the Amir of the Hajj, made up a crowd whose number is known to God alone. The vast plain (at Khulays) was filled with them, and the flat immensity of the desert was too narrow to encompass them. You could imagine the earth attempting to maintain its balance under the crowd's heaving and waves streaming from the force of its currents; you could picture in this crowd a sea swollen with waves, whose waters were the mirages and whose ships were the camels, their sails the lofty litters and round tents. They all went forward gliding in and out of a great rising of clouds of dust, their sides colliding as they passed. On the immense extent of the plain you could see the thrust of a crowd filled with pain and fright and the knocking together of litters. He who has not seen with his own eyes this Iraqi caravan has not experience one of the genuine marvels of the world worth the effort of describing and whose telling can seduce the listener by its marvelous character.
>
> "Consider what happens if one of the travellers assigned to a section of the caravan should have to leave it without taking note of a landmark to guide him back to his place. He would lose his way, would perish, and be reckoned among those lost in the desert. Occasionally distress of this type brings one of the travellers to the tent of the Amir to

request his assistance. The latter sends one of his information officers, one of those who have been appointed to pass on his orders, to find out the traveller's name, the name of his cameleer and of his country, and then to take him up behind him on his camel and make a circuit of the noisy mob. This officer announces all that in a loud voice, pointing out the lost person, giving the name of his cameleer and country until, perchance, the cameleer happens upon him and takes the man back into his own hands. If it does not happen that way that is the end of man's arrangement with his cameleer.

"Another marvelous thing about this caravan is that despite its huge size, which constitutes it a world unto itself, after the baggage has been unloaded and people are in their campsites, once the Amir has the drums called *kus* sounded to signal the departure, between that moment and the one when the camels are loaded with their packs, their saddles and their riders, the interval is no longer than the time it takes to twice say "No". Scarcely have they been sounded the third time and the animals are on the road. This is the result of firm planning and the detailed precautions that are taken for the trip.

"This caravan travels at night to the light of torches, which people on foot carry in their hands, and you will not see one litter which is not preceded by a torch. Thus people travel as it were among wandering stars which illuminate the depth of the darkness and which enable the earth to compare in brightness with the stars of heaven.[45]

As we shall see, Ibn Battuta came to Mecca with the Syrian caravan from Damascus; but he left eastward in the company of the Iraqi caravan headed across the *Darb Zubayda.* He writes:

"On the twentieth day of Dhu al-Hijja (17 November 1326) I went out of Mecca in company with the commander of the caravan of Iraq, the Pehlewan Muhammad al-Hawih, a man of Mossul, who occupied the office of commander of the pilgrims after the death of Shaykh Shihab al-Din Qalandar. Shihab al-Din was an open-handed and worthy man, who was held in high honor by his sultan, and used to shave his beared and eyebrows after the fashion of the Qalandars. When I left Mecca (God Most High ennoble her) in company with the above-mentioned Amir Pehlewan, he hired for me the half of a double litter as far as Baghdad, paying its cost from his own purse, and took me under his protection. We went out to the Bottom of Marr, after performing the farewell circuit with a host of men of Iraq, Khurasan, Fars and other eastern lands, of uncountable multitude, (so many that) the earth surged with them (as the sea surges) with dashing waves, and their advance was like the march of high-piled clouds. Anyone who left the caravan for natural want and had no mark by which to guide himself to his place could no find it again for the vast number of people. Included in this caravan were many water-carrying camels for the poorer pilgrims, who could obtain drinking water from them, and other camels to carry provisions (for distribution) as alms and to carry medicines, potions and sugar for those who should be attacked by illness. Whenever the caravan halted, food was cooked in great brass cauldrons, called *dasts,* and supplied from them to the poorer pilgrims and those who had no provisions. With the caravan were also a number of spare camels for the carriage of those unable to walk. All this was due to the benefactions and generosity of Sultan Abu Sa'id, Sultan of Morocco (1310-31). This caravan contained also animated bazaars and great supplies of luxuries and all kinds of food and fruit. They used to march during the night and light torches in front of the file of camels and litters, so that you saw the countryside gleaming with light and the darkness turned into radiant day."[45]

Caravans of the Mongols were also composed of the camels used to travel at night to avoid the heat of the day and also because the camels do not take fodder in the dark. "In the lands of the Mongols," informs Howorth, "when the approach of a caravan is announced the Mongols collect from all sides, greet the travelers with friendly phrases, and then proceed to question them vigorously about whence they came, wither they are bound, what merchandize they have with them, whether they have anything to sell, where and what price they have bought their camels etc. on the arrival of a caravan, it is especially after the camels have been loosened and the tents pitched that the strangers crowd in.[47] Caravans when entered a new place on their journey converted themselves into military formation so as to protect themselves from any danger of harassment or robbery. As Ibn Battuta tells that there was danger of despoiling by the Arab at Faid.[48] He had an engagement with the Afghans at Karmash (a mountainous tract to the south-east of Gardez), 35 miles east of Ghazna in which he separated from his party.[49]

There were lot of activities enroute and all kinds of danger and hardship faced by the caravans. Ibn Battuta gives us very interesting accounts of these journeys. At one place he writes: "the caravan stopped outside al-Karak for four days, at a place called al-Thaniya, and made preparations for entering the wilderness. Thence we traveled to Ma'an, which is the last town in Syria, and descended through the Pass of al-Sawan into the desert, of which the saying goes: 'He who enters it is lost, and he who leaves it is born'. After a march of two days we halted at Dhat Hajj, a place of subterranean water-beds with no habitations, then on to Wadi Baldah (but there is no water in it) , and then to Tabuk. This is the place, which was raided by the Apostle of God (God bless and give him peace) . It has a spring which used to yield a scanty supply of water, but when the Apostle of God (God bless and give him peace) went down to it and used it for his ablutions it give an abundant flow of running water and continues to do so to this day, through the blessed power of the Apostle of God (God bless and give him peace). It is the custom of the Syrian pilgrims, on reaching the camping ground of Tabuk, to take their weapons and unsheathe their swords, charge upon the camp and strike the palms with their swords, saying, "Thus did the Apostle of God (God bless and give him peace) enter it".

"The huge caravan encamps near the spring referred to, and every one of them slakes his thirst from it. They remain here for four days to rest themselves and tow after the camels and lay in supplies of water for the fearsome wilderness between Tabuk and al-Ula. It is the practice of the water-carriers to take up their positions at the sides of this spring, and they have tanks made of buffalo hides, like great reservoirs, from which they water the camels and fill the large water bags and ordinary water-skins. Each amir or person of rank has a (private) tank from which his camels and those of this retinue are watered, and their water-bags filled; the rest of the people arrange with the water carriers to water the camel and fill the water-skin of each person for a fixed sum of money.

"The caravan then sets out from Tabuk and pushes on speedily night and day, for fear of this wilderness. Halfway through is the valley al-Ukhaidir, which might well be the valley of Hell (God preserve us from it) . One year the pilgrims suffered severe distress in this place, by reason of the samoom- wind, which blows (there) , their water supplies dried up, and the price of a drink of water rose to a thousand dinars, but both seller and buyer perished. The story of this is inscribed on one of the rocks in the valley. (Going on) from there, the caravan halts at the Pool of al-Mu'azzam, a vast (basin), called after al-Malik al-Mu'azzam of the house of Ayyub, in which the rain- water collects in certain years but which is generally dry in others.

"On the fifth day after leaving Tabuk, they reach the well

of al-Hijr—the Hijr of Thamud—which has an abundance of water, but not one of the pilgrims draws of it, however, violent their thirst, following the example set by the Apostle of God (God bless and give him peace), when he passed it by on the expedition to Tabuk. For he drove on his riding camel, giving orders that none should water from it, and those who had used it to make dough fed their camels with it. At this place are the dwellings of Thamud, in some hills of red rock. They are hewn out and have carved thresholds, such that anyone seeing them would take them to be of recent construction. Their bones lie crumbling inside these houses 'verily, in that is a warning example'. The place of kneeling of the she-camel of Salih (on him be peace) is between two hills there, and in the space between them are the traces of a mosque, in which the pilgrims perform a prayer.

"From al-Hijr to al-'Ula is half a day's journey or less. Al 'Ula is a large and pleasant village with palm gardens and water springs at which the pilgrims half for the space of four nights. They provision themselves and wash their clothes, and also deposit here any surplus of provisions they may have, taking on with them only the amount of their strict necessities. The inhabitants of this village are trustworthy persons. This is the limit to which the Christian merchants of Syria may come, and beyond which they may not pass, and they trade in provisions and other goods with the pilgrims here.

"The caravan then sets out from al-'Ula and encamps on the day following the resumption of the journey in the valley known as al-'Itas (?). It is a place of violent heat, in which the fatal samoom-wind blows. It blew up one year on the caravan, and none but a few of the pilgrims escaped with their lives; that year is known as the year of the amir al-Jaliqi. After this they encamp at Hadiya, which is a place of sub-terranean waterbeds in a valley, they dig pits in it and the water comes up, but brackish. On the third day they alight outside the sanctified city (of al-Madina), the holy and illustrious."[50]

The success of the caravan trade required regular supplies of food and forage, some place to rest their animals enroute, a series of oasis, friendliness and the cordiality of the inhabitants, defence against marauders and safe line of communication. To take care of these requirements, there developed certain institutions like caravanserais, hospices or ribatat with regular supply of water and other necessities. The medieval rulers were aware of these hazards of travel and use to take up strong measures to maintain peace and security on the routes. Internal security and the safe movement of the travelling caravans were facilitated by constructing caravanserais or *ribatat* by the state, rich merchants or sometimes by the sufis.

Khan or caravanserai is a word of Persian origin designating a staging-post and lodging on the main communication routes, later a hostelry in the more important urban center. It had its roots in the beginning of organized highway trade in the earliest times, but it flourished with particular vigour in the Islamic world. The *Khan* was born of the need to ensure safe lodging and protection from robbery for travelers in regions where nomads and hill-bandits posed a threat to the security. It was an indispensable factor for commerce on the land and sea, necessary in regions where sources of provisions were not regular and where watering places were few and far between. It seems that it was originally an enclosure protecting a well, which in course of time developed into a work of architecture.[51]

The caravanserai was commonly constructed in the neighborhood, but not within the walls of a town or village. It was quadrangular in form with a dead wall outside; this wall had small windows high up; but in the lower parts merely a few narrow air holes. Inside a cloister-like arcade, surrounded by cellular storerooms, formed the ground floor, and a somewhat higher arcade, giving access to little dwelling rooms, runs around it above. Broad open flights of stone steps connected the stories. The central court used to be opened to sky, and generally had in its center a well with a fountain basin beside it. A spacious gateway, high and wide enough to admit the passage of a loaded camel, formed the sole entrance, which was furnished with heavy doors and was further guarded within by massive iron chains, drawn across at night. The entry was paved with flagstones, and there were stone seats on each side. The court itself was generally paved, and large enough to contains 300 or 400 crouching camels or tethered mules; the bales of merchandise were piled away under the lower arcade, or stored in the cellars behind it. The upstairs apartments were for human lodging; cooking was usually carried on in one or more corners of the quadrangle below. Should the caravansarai be a small one, the merchants and their goods alone found place within the beasts of burden being left outside. Many caravansarai had considerable architectural merit; their style of construction was in general that known as Saracenic; their massive walls were of hewn stone; their proportions apt and grand. The portals especially were often decorate with intricate carving; so also in the prayer niche within.[52]

Hudud al Alam is full of references to caravansarai.[53] Al-Muqaddassi also mentions caravansarai or inns throughout the regions in his times. A city in Central Asia named Isbijah was an important one, well developed, having an inn for merchants and a market for the cotton merchant.[54] It was the duty of the state to facilitate the merchants by the building of ribats and caravansarais. The Saljuq rulers exemplified themselves with the great protector of the merchant class and they got built caravansarais throughout their kingdom. Qavurt after suppressing Baluchi brigands put watch- towers, cisterns and caravansarais along the caravan route through the desert to Siestan as early as in the second half of the eleventh century.[55] Malik Shah when visited Baghdad and made the city his winter capital, a great mosque, markets and caravanserai were built there in AD 1091-92.[56]

According to *Safar-Nama* of Nasir-i-Khusrau, there were fifty good caravansarai in Isfahan in his day where the merchants congregated and had rooms.[57] Yakut, tells us that he had never seen the prosperity in urban and agricultural fields as in Khwarizm and highly speaks of the caravansarai and mosques of Samarqand (58). A suburb built by Rashiduddin Fazlullah in Tabriz had 24 caravansarais, 1500 shops, bath houses, gardens, mills, workshops for paper-making and dye-works etc.[59] Persian architecture in buildings including caravansarais during medieval period is worth noticeable.[60]

The Turks gave direct encouragement to visiting merchants in other ways than the provision of trade treaties. They worked hard to resettle the land and initiated vigorous building programmes in the towns. By the early thirteenth century Konya and Sivas were flourishing meeting places for Italians merchants, for Indian merchants and, occasionally, for the Greeks of Trebizond and the Muslims of Syria and Egypt. *Khans* or caravansarais were built at the main stopping points along the classical Anatolian trade routes.[61]

Caravansarais, which were also called *funduqs*, played an important role in the international trade. Some *khans* were constructed for particular groups of foreign traders, such as Maghribis, Persians or European. A caravansarai for Syrian merchants built in the twelfth century had 360 lodgings above the storerooms and enough space for 4000 guests at a time.[62]

The institution of constructing caravansarais continued in the later years also. A rich merchant of Yazd, one Haji Mirza Hussein erected a caravansarai in 1896 A.D. at his own expenses. It was called *Rabat-i-gur*, the wild Asses' caravanserai, which was well built of burnt bricks mostly from the ruins of older caravansarais in the neighbour-hood. A modern traveller who visited this caravansarai informs us that the purpose was the custom of purchasing the salvation after death by the erection of such structures. It had counterpart in other countries also.[63] The caravansarais were locked at night for the protection of the merchandize.[64]

In Ottoman Empire the caravansarais were built for different groups of foreign merchants. For example, in a city called Bursa different caravansarais were reserved for the caravan from Iran where their silk bales were weighed and scale tax was paid.[65] In the province of Anatolia, there were seventy-five caravansarais, the rent of which was the part of the revenue of the province.[66]

For small groups of travelers, traders or individuals there were hospices or hostelries, lodging rooms or *khanqahs* built either by state or individuals for welfare purposes. These hospices played a significant role in the medieval trade and commerce. Al-Muqaddasi mentions small lodging rooms with windows looking out over the street in the capital of Bukhara called Numujkath.[67] At another place he refers a hospice built by one Nasir bin Ahmad with accommodation for the wayfarers.[68]

In the travel account of Marco Polo we find good description of the hostelries enroute to China specially Cathay (Beijing), the capital. He mentions twelve gates of the city and out side every gate was a suburb and these suburbs were so great that they contained more people than the city itself. In those suburbs lodged the foreign merchants and travelers. There were in each of the suburbs, to distance of a mile from the city, numerous fine hostelries for the lodgment of merchants from different parts of the world, and a special hostelry was assigned to each description of people, as if would say there was one for the Lombard, another for the German, and a third for the Frenchmen.[69] At another place he informs that every hostler who kept a hostel for travelers was bound to register their names and surnames, as well as the day and month of their arrival and departure.[70]

Ibn Battuta during his journey through Iraq, Persia,

Turkistan and Khurasan, witnessed large numbers of caravanserais and hospices in every town. The hospices were of small structure with lodging facilities for the travelers not as big as the caravanserais. It appears from his account, the hospices were generally owned by an individual who were pious and devotee persons like Sheikhs and Sufis. He made note of certain women who also held hospices and extended hospitality to the travelers. He and his party enjoyed the facilities and hospitalities at a number of hospices especially on their route from Khwarizm to Delhi onwards.

The first city visited by Ibn Battuta was Khwarizm (modern Khiva) . It was at that time the longest, greatest, most beautiful and most important city of the Turks having fine bazaars and broad streets, a great number of buildings and abundance of commodities. Outside the city was a hospice built over the tomb of the Sheikh Najmal-Din al-Kubra, who was one of the great saints of his times. Food was supplied in it to all wayfarers and its Sheikh was the teacher at the college named Saif al-Din ibn Asaba, one of the principal citizens of Khwarizm. In the town there was also a hospice, where Sheikh was the pious Jalaluddin al-Samarqandi one of the most saintly men. He received Ibn Battuta and his party hospitably in it.[71] Ibn Battuta refers one hospice built by one Turabak, wife of the governor of the city of Khwarizm. She gave a banquet in the honour of our Moroccan traveller for which she assembled the doctors of the laws and the principal citizens. This was held in this hospice. The food was supplied to all wayfarers in hospice as witnessed by him.[72]

The next reference of a hospice by Ibn Battuta is in the suburbs of Bukhara called Fath Abad . It had the tomb of the learned Sheikh and pious ascetic Saif al-Din al-Bakharzi. This hospice was a large institution with vast endowments from which food was supplied to all corners and its supervisor was a descendant of the Sheikh's family. Yahya al-Bakharzi entertained Ibn Battuta at his residence. He invited all the leading men of the city on this occasion. The Koran readers recited with beautiful modulations and sang melodiously in Turkish and Persian.[73]

It seems from Juvaini's account that this hospice was, funded by the mother of great Khans Mangu and Kubilai although she herself was a Christian. He writes, "And her hand was ever open in munificence and benefaction, and although she was a follower and devotee of the religion of Jesus she would bestow alms and presents upon *imams* and *sheikhs* and strove also to revive the sacred observances of the faith of Muhammad. And the token and proof of this statement is that she gave 1000 silver *balish* that a college (*madrasa*) might be built in Bokhara, of which pious foundation the *Sheikh-al-Islam* Saifuddin of Bakhraz should be administrator and superintendent; and commanded that villages should be bought, an endowment made and teachers and students accommodated (in the college) ."[74]

From Bukhara, Ibn Battuta reached at a placed called Nakhshab (Nasaf) about hundred miles south-east of Bukhara and a main station on the old route through Iran gate to Tirmiz and Balkh. There he with one of his slave girl lodged outside it in a house that belonged to its governor.[75]

Reaching in the outskirts of Samarqand he tells about a tomb of Qutham having a hospice. It had chambers for the lodging of travellers. The tomb was visited by the people of Samarqand on the eve of every Tuesday and Friday; the Tatars too used to come to visit it and to seek the blessings of the saint did not injure in anyway the condition of this site; on contrary, they used to visit it to gain the blessing as the result of the miraculous signs which they witnessed on its behalf. According to him, they made large votive offerings to it, bringing cattle, sheep, dirham and dinars, all of which was devoted to expenditure for the maintenance of travellers and survivors of the hospice and the tomb. Being a large endowment, it was looked after by a superintendent appointed by sultan Tarmashirin.[76]

The old city of Tirmiz was built on the bank of the Jayhun

and when it was laid waste by the Mongols, the new city was built two miles from the river. The lodging of Ibn Battuta and his party was arranged in the hospice of the pious Sheikh Azizan, one of the great and most generous sheikhs. He possessed great wealth and house property and orchards and spent his wealth to supply the needs of travelers.[77]

After crossing the river Jayhun, their entered the land of Khurasan and reached Balkh which was completely dilapidated and unihabitated. Here he noticed a beautiful mosque, hospice opposite a convent (for sufi devotees) which were built by a woman whose husband was the governor of the city for the Abbasid Caliphs named Daud b. Ali.[78]

Resuming their journey from the city of Balkh, Ibn Batluta and his party traveled for seven days through the mountains of Quhistan (lying to the west of Balkh). There were many inhabited villages on the way in which there were running streams and leafy trees and many hospices inhabited by pious devotees. Ibn Battuta does not mention whether he stayed any of these hospices or not and straightway mentions his arrival at Herat.[79]

From Herat, our Moroccan friend reached a place called al-Jam, a place of middle size, pretty with orchards and trees, abundance of springs and flowing streams. He relates a story of Abu Said, the Sultan of al-Iraq who had come to Khurasan on one occasion and encamped in the city, in which was the hospice of Shaikh Ahmad. This Shaikh entertained the Sultan with immense display of hospitality. He gave one sheep to every tent in the Sultan's *mahalla,* one sheep to every four men. To every riding beast, whether horse, mule or ass, one night's forage was given so that not a single animal was left in the *mahalla* without receiving its share of his hospitality.[80]

From al-Jam the party reached Tus, where he mention a hospice with a college and a mosque adjoining it. All these buildings were of elegant construction, their walls being colourfully decorated with Qashani titles.[81] From Tus he reached Naisabur via the cities of Sarakhs and Zawa. Naisabur was one of the four metropolitan cities of Khurasan. It was called sometimes, 'Little Damascus' because of its quantities of fruits, orchards and streams and by reason of its beauty. The city had a hospice where Ibn Battuta lodged himself. It belonged to one Qutub al Din al-Naisaburi. He extended to our traveler excellent and most generous hospitality and also shown some miracles.[82]

From Naisabur they went to the city of Bistam where Ibn Battuta's lodging was in a hospice of Shaikh Abu Yazd al-Bistami.[83] He continued his journey from the city by way of Hindukhir (100 miles west of Balkh) to Qunduz and Baghlan, which were regions of villages where they were to be found Shaikhs and pious men with fruit-gardens and streams. Ibn Battuta with his party encamped at Qunduz by a flowing river where there was a hospice belonging to one of the Shaikhs of the poor brethren, an Egyptian who called *Shir Siyah,* means 'The Black Lion'. There the party was entertained by the governor of that land, living in a large garden, thereabout. Ibn Battuta and his party remained on the outskirts of this village for about forty days, in order to pasture the camels and horses. The other reason for their halt was the fear of snow.[84]

On setting out from Baghlan they journeyed to a place called Andar (Andarab on the headwaters of River Surkhab. The valley of Andrab leads to the Khawak Pass 13,000 feet) . The party alighted in a large village in which there was a hospice belonging to an excellent man named Muhammad al-Mahrawi. They lodged with him who treated them with consideration. He would drink the water in which the travelers had washed their hands after eating, because of his strong belief and his benevolence. He traveled with Ibn Battuta until they scaled the mountain of Hindukush.[85]

The next reference of a hospice we find at Ghazni. It was in ruined condition at that time when Ibn Battuta made a halt with his party. He was honourably received by the governor Mardak Agha meaning 'little man of great family'. The hospice was with the tomb of Mahmud, but no facilities available there.[86]

The party next traveled to Kabul where a hospice of one Sheikh Ismail al-Afghani, the disciple of Sheikh Abbas, was located. But Ibn Battuta does not mention whether he and his party stayed over there or not.[87] From there onwards Ibn Battuta rode to Karmash and then to Shashnagar the last inhabited place on the confines of the land of the Turks and from there to Attock and thence to Indus, where he finds a well-organized system of intelligence service and arrangements for the travellers,[88]

For any commercial development a warm reception from the targetted populace plays the key role. To create a wide acceptability all markets, friendly benefits have to be provided. And this was fairly well done for the medieval merchant classes. Hence, a rare blend of these commescial networks of road, growing facilites for the trading communities such as caravansarais and hospices throughout the Asian kingdoms paved the way for the growth of towns and markets and to create business friendly and at home circumstances in which moved the medieval diaspora with their goods withont any fear. It also determined the revival of silk route which again had become the first love of entire people.

The towns, cities and markets of Central Asia had always attracted the merchants to exploit their economic and commercial advantages. They used to approach these cities to load and unload different commodities in the markets for further destination either to China or to India or the west. These cities being situated on the silk road were connected with almost whole region of Asia and Europe and were providing well established institution of caravanserais, markets and other facilities required by the different trading communities from different lands as already highlighted. To aroid any repetion we are coneerned only with the major crities or towns of central Asia.

SAMARQAND

Samarqand was one of the leading cities of Central Asia having all facilities and requirements for the merchants visiting and lodged in it. It was as a center of international trade during this period. It was situated on the bank of the river called Wadi'l-Qassarin, along which there were norias to supply water to the orchards. *Hudud al Alam* being an earlier source of our information places Samarqand on the heights and announces that the city was well connected through roads and rivers with towns in Central Asian and Persia. It had been a resort of merchants from all over the world. There are references of various groups of people living near by a large village known as Samarqandaq (little Samarqand) which included Hindus, Tibetans and Muslims etc. It has been described as a large, prosperous and a very pleasant town, having a citadel, a monastery, a suburb and stream of water flowing besides the city. It produced paper which was exported all over the world.[89]

The paper of Samarqand had driven out of use the Egyptian papyrus and the parchment which previous generations employed; that was because it looked better, was more supple, was more easily handled and was more convenient for writing on. On the basis of the author of the *Kitab al-masalik wal-mamalik* 'Book of roads and province', the Chinese prisoners of war captured by Ziyad b. Salih and brought to Samarqand were some artisans who manufactured papers in Samarqand; then it was manufactured on a wide scale and passed into general use, until it became an important export commodity for the people of Samarqand. Its value was universally recognized and people everywhere used it. Further, specialties of Samarqand were ampanomiac, Wadhari- textiles, mercury, hazel-nuts and slaves. Tabir b. Abdallah b. Tahir once issued an instruction to his agents, 'If you ever come across a Tukharistan draught horse, a Bardha's mule, an Egyptian ass or a Samarqand slave then buy it immediately and don't bother referring back to me for a decision'.[90] The she-camels of Samarqand were famous for cross-breeding as they had two humps with good temperaments as told by al-Idrisi.[91]

The Persian chroniclers reveal that when Chinghiz and his troops occupied Samarqand in AD 1220, they spared thirty thousand of its artisans and engineers who were sent to Mongolia, which shows the significance of the city as a great center of manufacturing of different articles.[92] In the medieval Chinese literature there are many references of Samarqand. It was more than a thousand *li* and was called Sun-sz-kan, which means fat, and, as the land there was very fertile, the city received this name. To quote *Si Yu Lu,* "The country is very rich and populous. They have gold and copper coins, but their coins are not provided with a hole, nor have they rims (as the Chinese copper coins have) . Around the city, to an extent of several tens of *li,* there are everywhere orchards, groves, flower gardens, aqueducts, running springs, square basins, and round ponds in uninterrupted succession; indeed, Sun-sz-kan is a delicious place! The watermelons there are as large as a horse's head. Regarding grain and vegetables, however, the *shu,* the *no,* and the *ta-tou* are not found there (*Shu* is a glutinous varieties of the common millet, *no* is rice, peculiar to Eastern Asia and *ta–tou* soy bean). It does not rain there in summer. People make wine from grapes. There are mulberry trees, but not fit for the breeding of silkworms. All cloths are made of *ku-sun* (probably cotton) . White colour for cloth is considered as a good omen, whilst black is the mourning colour. Wherefore all clothes seen there are white (the Chinese consider white as the mourning colour) ."[93]

A Chinese traveller Chang Chun and his party who reached Samarqand on December 2, 1221, after crossing a great river (The river was crossed at Zarafshan) , where they met in the suburb, first councilor of the emperor, the chief officer of the Mongol army and having pitched great number of tents, they rested there. About Samarqand he wrote "is laid out on the borders of canals. As it never rains in summer and autumn, the people have constructed two rivers in the city and distributed the water through all the streets, so that every house can make use of it. Before the dynasty of the *Suan-tuan* (Sultan of Khwarizm) was overthrown, the city of Samarqand had a population of more than a hundred thousand families but after the occupation only the fourth part remained behind. Most of the fields and gardens belong to the Mohammedans, but they are not allowed to dispose of them. They are obliged to manage their properties in on junction with Ki-tan (i.e. Karakhitai) , Chinese, and men from Ho si (Chinese name for Tangut empire partly subdued by Chinghiz in 1218) . Chinese workmen are living everywhere. In the middle of the city there is an elevated place about a hundred feet high, on which the new palace of the Sultan was built. . . . We saw there, peacocks and great elephants, which had come from Yin-du (India) , a country situated several thousand *li* to the south-east."[94]

Chang Te, a courier of Mongke Khan, who was sent to Hulegu Khan in Persia arrived Samarqand on April 1, 1259, which was a very large and populous. According to his travel account *Si Shi Ki*, at that time a great many flowers were in bloom. Among the plants of that country only roses were the same as in China other flowers were unknown. West of the city of Samarqand people cultivated vines, the common rice, and wheat. The author admires the medicinal plants produced there, unknown in China, and very efficacious in curing diseases. He makes special reference to the *a-rh-dji* which cured the ulcers of horses. It was also useful in cases of wounds and in the prevention of miscarriage. Taking a dose the size of a bean and swallowing it, the patient would recover.[95] The account of Minhaj discloses that Samarqand and Bukhara were great marts from where Mongke Khan through his officials purchases 80,000 horses in less than a week.[96] Marco Polo's account refers Samarqand as a great and noble city inhabited by both Christians and Muslims.[97]

On the basis of the earlier writings, Mustawfi informs, "The city of Samarqand is like heaven for greenness, her palaces are like stars for grandeur, her river is like the milky- way for breadth, her wall is like the path of the Sun (in the eclipse) . Samarqand occupies a plain in which stand the city and the citadel and a number of villages; and this plain formerly was enclosed by a wall, 50,000 paces in circumference, some parts of this wall still existing down to the present day. In ancient times a mighty castle had been built in the lands of this plain, but it fell to ruin. Then at the time, when the world-famed hero, Karshaf came thither, a part of the ruins of this castle was thrown down by an earthquake and a treasure was discovered. Karshaf with that treasure built the castle in good condition, but after a time it again fell to ruin. Then Gushtasf son of Luhrasf the Kayanian restored its buildings, giving the castle strong fortifications and a mighty deep ditch and he built a wall to stand between Turkistan and the plains of that country, as a barrier between Iran and Turan, the length of which was 20 circumference leagues. Next Alexander the Great found in this plain a mighty city whose 12,000 paces. After his days in the time of the Kings of the Tribes (the Parthiams) one Samar by name, who was of the race of the Tubba's of Yaman, by reason of his enmity against the people of that land, laid this city in ruins and razed it (*bi-kand*) to the ground level to so that no building remained standing; hence they called it Samarqand (Samar hath razed it), which the Arabs in Arabic wrote as Samarqand. The climate of this country is cold. Its waters come from the river. By and from the Barash and Barmash channels, and great canals traverse the plain all round and about the city along with numerous gardens have been laid out. Sughd of Samarqand, which is one of the most famous pleasure grounds of the world, lies along this river, whose stream in spring-time carries many boats. The produce of the land is corn and much fruit, of its fruits being grapes, apples and melons, all of excellent quality. The population is of the sects of the Hanafites and Shafites."[98] At another place while discussing the different metals he informs us that the mountains of Samarqand had mines of gold and silver which were easily worked and gave good gold and silver.[99]

The people of Samarqand were great travellers who took their journeys to distant lands. According to Rashiduddin Fazllullah the people of Samarqand had made a colony in the north-west of Peking where they had planted a number of gardens in the Samarqand style.[100] Ibn Battuta though skipped many of these details, provides us a good account of the city. According to him Samarqand was one of the greatest and finest cities. It was built on the bank of river called Wadi'l-Qassarin, along which there were norias to supply water to the orchards. The residents of Samarqand were fond of walking near the river where benches and seats were provided. Stalls were opened for selling fruits and other edibles. He speaks of a palace, which fell before the onslaught of the Mongols, and at the time of his visit no city walls or gates could be seen except gardens. He was highly influenced by the generous qualities of the people of Samarqand who were always affectionate towards the strangers and better than the people of Bukhara. He mentions a tomb of one Qutham, which had a hospice. It was visited by the inhabitants of the city, and the Mongols. Large offerings were brought which included sheep, cattle, dirhams, diners, etc. The hospice had a number of chambers as pointed out earlier, to lodge travelers. He admires the Mongols for the maintenance of this structure, which was beautifully decorated with golden jewel.[101]

Yakut speaks of the double gates of iron in Samarqand. The city proper had four gates, namely *Bab-as-Sin* (the China gate) , to the east, to which steps ascended from the lower level. The Bukhara Gate, to the north; to the west the *Bab-an-Nau-Bahar,* and to the south the *Bab-al-Kabir* (the Great Gate) , also known as the Kish Gate. The great market place of Samarqand was called the *Ras-at-Tak*, "Head of the Arch" and was a fine square. The markets in the suburb all converged on the square of the *Ras-at-Tak* in the city, and all the road-ways paved with stone flags. The markets in the suburbs were the center of trade full of merchandise and the merchants from all parts, for the city was the great emporium of Transoxiana.[102] Ahmad Ibn Arabshah states Samarqand as one of the more notable cities and famous place of Transoxiana, the walls of which formally, according to popular account, were of twelve *parsangs* in length and that from the time of Jalaluddin.[103]

The glory and the splendour of Samarkqand reached to its height when Timur made it as his capital. The Spanish ambassador Clavijo (AD 1405) praised the city finding new buildings, mosques and caravanserais. Timur had spared no efforts to beautify and enrich the city of Samarkand. It became a large emporium for products and manufactured goods, for the lord of Central Asia obliged artisans of all trade to settle in the capital. "Many merchants" writes Clavijo, "Turks, Arabs, Moors of diverse sects with Christians who were Greek and Armenians . . . besides Indians trade there, for the markets of Samarkand are amply stored with merchandise imported from distant or foreign countries, such as Russia, Tartars, China and India. The goods included leather, linens, silk-stuffs, precious stones, unguents, herbs, spices, preservers with special emphasis on Chinese products which were regarded as the richest and most precious of all those brought thither from foreign parts, for the craftsmen of Cathay are reputed to be the most skilful by far beyond those of any other nation." The Spanish ambassador also mentions an eight hundred camel caravanserais bringing merchandise from China, which just preceded him to Samarqand.4

Later we find Babur so fascinated with the beauty of Samarqand that he mentions, "Few towns in the whole habitable world are so pleasant as this city." He ordered people to pace round the ramparts of the walled-town, which came out at 10000 steps. Samarqandis were all orthodox, pure-in-the Faith, law-abiding and religious. About its location he writes "On the east of Samarqand are Farghana and Kashghar; on the west Bukhara and Khwarizm; on the north, Tashkint and Shahrukhiya—in books written Shash and Banakat, and on the south Balkh and Tirmiz. Among its fruits were grapes, melons, apples, pomegranates, etc. which were of good quality. He also refers to number of fine buildings and gardens built by Timur and his successors in the town and its suburbs. He mentions one Friday mosque of stone, on that worked many stone-cutters, brought from Hindustan. At another place he describes Samarqand as a wonderfully beautified town. One of its specialities, perhaps found in few other places, was that the different traders were not mixed up together in it but each had its own bazaar, a good sort of plan. It bakers and its cooks were good where each trade had its own bazaars. It produced the best paper in the world and also cramoisy velvet, which was carried to other countries. He also praises the meadows around Samarkand.[105]

Bukhara

Next to Samarqand was Bukhara which was a large and prosperous town of Transoxiana since earlier centuries. During tenth century it had been the seat of the king of the East called *Malik-I-Mashriq.* It produced plenty of fruit and had running-water system. Among commercial commodities the town of Bukhara exported woolen carpets and saltpeter to different regions. There was a wall built around the city in which, were located number of *ribats.*[106]. Another account for the same period refers to a number of gates, one was called the gate of spice merchant probably to be sought for the east side of the town allowing spices from India.[107] In a *waqfnama* (a legal letter stipulating a charitable endownment) of 1326, Indians are mentioned alongside Turks, Tajiks and Mongols as visitors to a Bukharan *khanqah* or Sufi hostel.[108]

Among the Chinese medieval travelers Ye-Lu Chu Tsai places Bukhara to the west of Samarqand at a distance of six or seven hundred *li* and informs, "it abounds in every kind of products, and a richer than Samarqand. There is the residence of the *so-li-tan* of the *Mou-su-lu-man* (Mussulman) people. The cities of *K'u-djan* (Khodjend) and *O-ta-la* (Otrar) , and others all depend on *Pu hua* (Bukhara) .[109] When Ibn Battuta reached Bukhara, he found the city and its bazaars, mosque, college all in ruins, all but a few, and its inhabitants were looked down upon and their evidence (in legal cases) was not accepted in Khwarizm or elsewhere, because of their reputation for factionalism, and making false claims, and denial of truth. There was not a single person in the city who possessed any religious bearing.[110]

In *Nuzhat-al-Qulub* we notice that Bukhara had silver-mines and in the mountains near the city, copper-mines. There were mines of turquoise in the mountains lying between Bukhara and Ushrusanah. It also mentions a spring of asphalt (Qir) near Bukhara.[111] At another place it tells that Bukhara was one of the famous cities of Transoxiana and in former times had a circular wall, the diameter of which was twelve leagues, and from Bukhara to Samarkand, an eight days journey along the river- bank was full of gardens.[112]

A *waqfnama* mentions a place in Bukhara known as the 'Hill of the Indians', which reflect the multinational importance of the city as a center of trade.[113]

In later period Babur also gives us a noticeable account of Bukhara, which according to him, was the largest district, and one that was its equal, was Samarqand. It was a fine town; its fruits were many and good; its melons excellent, none in Mawarannahr matching them for quality and quantity. The Bukhara plum was famous and without equal. Dried plums with the skins removed were taken from province to province.

Medicinally it was an excellent laxative. Throughout Transoxiana no wine was strong than Bukhara wines. When Babur was at Samarqand, he tasted Bukhara wine.[114]

According to Vambery, Bukhara was not merely luxurious, it was also principal emporium for the trade between China and Western Asia, in addition to the vast warehouses for silks, brocades and cotton stuffs, for the finest carpets and all kinds of gold and silversmith's work; it boasted a great money-market, being the exchange of all the populations of Eastern and Western Asia; and there is a proverb current to this day 'As wide awake as a broker of Bokhara'.[115]

Kish

Two days journey from Samarkand was located Kish on the Samarkand—Tirmiz highway. W. Barthold while discussing the sources of the pre-Mongol period mentions two works dealing with the history of Kish and Nasaf which shows how significant was the city of Kish.[116] The town of Kish, known as *shahr-i-sabz*, was once regarded, if Yakubi is to be believed, as the most important town in Soghd. In the Samanid period it was falling into decay, which is to be attributed to the rise of Samarkand and Bukhara. The *shahristan* had four gates: Iran Gate, Gate of Ubaydallah, Gate of the Butchers and Gate of the inner city. In the Samanid period the *shahristan* and citadel were in ruins and the only part of it was the *rabid*, with two gates. The climate of Kish was considered to be very unhealthy. Ibn Hauqal enumerates sixteen districts in the province of Kish.[117]

Hudud al-Alam mentions Kish as a borough belonging to the hot zone, falling much rain in it. It possessed a city, a citadel, and a suburb. Two rivers flowing past the town gate were used in the fields. In the mountains were found mines of drugs. The city produced good mules, manna (*tarangabin*) , and red salt, which was exported everywhere.[118]

A Chinese official speaks about an island of Kish, people of which were white and clean and eight feet tall. They wore their hair loose under a turban eight feet long, one half of which hung down their back. They made use of gold and silver coins. The food consisted of wheaten cakes, mutton, fish and dates. They did not eat rice. The country of Kish produced pearls and fine horses.

In the year AD 1255, Hulegu Khan spent a pleasant month at Kish as told by Juvaini.[119] In later years, Kish being the birth place of Timur, attained fame, who gave attention to the city and rebuilt it where the white palace Ak-Saray became his favourite place of residence. It was during this period that the city took its name as *Shahr-i-sabz*, "the Green City."[130] Mustawfi too mentions Kish as one of the important cities of Transoxiana.[121]

Babur also took notice of Kish and confirms that Timur tried hard to make it his capital being his birth-place. He erected noble buildings in it and to seat his own court he built a great arched hall and also for those attending the court he built two smaller halls and to seat petitioners to his court while small recesses on the four sides of the court house. He also got built in Kish a college and a mausoleum in which were the tombs of Jahangir Mirza and his other descendants. Kish was called *Shahr-i-Subz* because its barren wastes and roofs and walls became beautifully green in spring. But Kish did not offer the same facilities as Samarkand for becoming a town and a capital. Timur at last made a clear choice of Samarkand.[122]

Marv

Classical sources refer to the Murghab as the Margus river and to the region of Marv as Margiana. Authors like Pliny attribute the foundation of the city to Alexander. During this period, a wall was built to protect the agricultural zone from the nomads of the steppe, and then inhabited by the predecessor of the Turkish people. Agricultural was highly developed which shows that the valley of the Murghab had a system of artificial irrigation. The rapid development of the oasis of Marv was due not only to this but also to the fact that in the Parthian period the great caravan route which linked Western Asia with China passed through Marv. The caravan from western Asia went from Merv to Balkh, thence via the Darwaz and the northern part of Badakshan, then on to the Alay, Kashghar and finally to China. In the Sasanid period, the trade route was moved further north. Caravans went from Marv to Cardjuy, Samarkand and Semirecye or the land of the Seven Rivers. Marv was not only an emporium on the trade route but a great industrial city. It is, however, only after the Arab conquest that history gives us ample details of the life of the city.[123]

Marv had been a large town as told by the author of *Hudud al-Alam* where the *mir* of Khurasan had his residence. It was a pleasant and flourishing place with a citadel with numerous castles. It had been the abode of the Sasanian kings. There was no better town in all Khurasan than Marv. Its markets were good. It produced good cotton, root of asafoetida, *filata-sweets,* vinegar, condiments, textiles of raw silk and *mulham* silk.[124] While describing the Chinese medieval map Bretschneider mentions Marv or Merv as MA-LI-WU which was marked on the ancient map south of Bukhara and evidently denoted it one of the four capitals (Merv, Herat, Nishapur, Balkh) of Khurasan in the middle age. It was one of the places of abundance of Zendavesta. On the basis of Arab geographers' writings Merv distinguished two cities of this name, one of which was called *Meru Shahidjan* the other *Meru-al-Rud.* Both were situated on the river *Meru-rud,* called a *Murghb.*[125]

Marv had played important role in the economic life of Western Asia and Central Asia, as reflected in the writings of the Arab geographers, i.e. Ibn Hawkal and al-Muqqaddasi. It was to thirteenth century that the great economic prosperity of the oasis of Marv belongs, with a highly developed system of exchanges. Numerous technical and agricultural methods of cultures were developed, except the cultivation of wheat, which was imported from the valleys of Kashka-Darya and Zarafshan. The people cultivated the silk worm. Shortly before the coming of the Mongols there was at Kharak to the south-west of Marv a "house" called Diwakush where sericulture was studied. Al-Istakhri says that Marv exported the most raw silk; its silk factories were celebrated. The oasis was also famous for its fine cotton which was exported, raw or manufactured, to different lands.[126] The Arabs used to call all thick and coarse cloths brought from Khurasan *Marawi,* and all finally woven ones, *Shahajani,* for they considered Merv to be the focal point of Khurasan and the city was called Merv ash-Shahajan; "to this day", mentions *Lata if al-maarif,* "all fine garments are called *Shahajani.*" The specialities of Merv included cloths woven with a gold thread (*mulham*) . The city was famous for four products beginning with letter *mim* which were sent as presents to other lands. These were—mulham (cloth); mulabban, (confectionery); *murri,* (brine) (for pickling and also used medicinally) and *makanis,* (sweeping brushes). In praise of Merv, the same source mentions:

A healthy spot, abundant running water and earth whose sweetness surpasses even that of subtly compounded perfume!

Whenever a man plans to depart from there, its very name prevents him from leaving (ma-ru-*in Persian,* 'do not go'!) [127]

The district of Marv also contained a number of large estates, which assured their owners considerable revenue. The city developed rapidly with its manufacturers, markets and agriculture. Marv became in the 5th/11th century a commercial city of the regular oriental type. It was traversed by two main streets one running north and south the other east and west; where they intersected was the *carsu,* the center of the market, roofed by a dome; the shops had flat roofs. It was there also that were to be found the little shops of the artisans and although the literary sources only mention the money-changers, the goldsmiths' and the tanner' quarters, there also must have been the quarters of the weavers, coppersmiths, potters etc. It was not only the administrative and religious center, for it also contained the palaces, the mosques, madrasas and other buildings. According to Yakut to the north of *carsu* was the great mosque which survived till the Mongol invasion. He spent two years in the libraries of Marv before the Mongol cataclysm.[128]

Juvaini opens his account on Marv and the fate there of "Marv was the residence of Sultan Sanjar and the rendezvous of great and small. In extent of territory it excelled among the lands of Khorasan, and the bird of peace and security flew over its confines. The number of its chief men rivalled the drops of April rain and its earth contended with the heavens; its *dihqans*, from the greatness of their riches, breathed the breath of equality with the monarchs and emirs of the age and set down the foot of parity with the mighty and haughty ones of the world.

A fair land a merciful lord, and a soil whose clay bleeds ambergris;
And when a man prepares to depart therefrom, by its very name it forbids him to depart.[129]

Juvaini also gives in details the destruction of the city, massacre of the people except the artisans[130] Mustawfi in the mid-fourteenth century found Marv largely in ruins.[131]

KASGHAR-YARKAND-KHOTAN

The commercial network will be incomplete without making mention of a well-knit tri-knot of Kashghar-Yarkand and Khotan. This was the easternmost link on the historical Silk Route. This triangle has been referred collectively in the contemporary literature available to us. Mustawfi is one who writing in the fourteenth century informs that Khotan was a kingdom, Kashghar and Yarkand were its celebrated towns.[132]

Hudud al Alam an earliest account of the tenth century makes no mention of Yarkand. However, about Khotan it tells this region was located between the rivers. In its limits lived *mardumand vahshi mardumkhwar* (man-eaters). The commodities of the inhabitants were mostly raw silk. The king of Khotan during that period was called *azim al–Turk wal–Tubat* (Lord of the Turks and Tibetans) and lived in a great *hayat* (state) on the boundary of china and Tibbet. He had eunuchs in charge of all his districts. That land turned out 70,000 warriors. According to the author jade stone came from the rivers of Khotan.[133]

The Chinese sources styled Khotan as *Yu-t'ien* which gave the sound 'jade,' a highly prized stone in China. The name Khotan came to be known under the Mongol rule. Thirteen waters-stations on the rivers were established by an imperial order between the two cities Khotan and Yarkand. The people of Khotan were relieved from the onus of collecting jade for the emperor. Khotan was famous in the West for its musk in addition to jade.[134]

Marco Polo gives separate account of these three towns. About Khotan he mentions that it was a province which, was eight days' journey in extent and was subject to the Great Khan. The inhabitants were Muhammdens. The province had plenty of cities ad towns. He makes it clear that Khotan bore the name of kingdom as well as the capital which, was a splendid city, amply stocked with the means of life. Cotton grew there in plently. the people were peace loving and lived by trade and industry.[135]

As far Kashghar is concerned Marco Polo describes it as the biggest town and the most splendid city. The inhabitants lived by trade and industry. They had fine orchards and vineyards and flourishing states. Cotton grew there in plenty besides flax and hemp. The soil was fruitful and productive of all the means of life. He does not confirm whether Kashghar was a city or province. However, he states that the country was the starting point from which many merchants set out to market their wares all over the world.[136]

About Yarkand Marco Polo is the one who leaves a little account of the province and reforms us that this was five days' journey in extent. The inhabitant were Muhammdens and were subject to the great Khan' nephew Kaidu. It was amply stocked with the means of life, especially cotton. Our European friend does not find much worth metioning about Yarkand.[137]

One can suggest that the tri-kont was serving as the trading centers and seems to be the capitals of the respective provinces. The contemporaries are little silent may be bcacuse of their insignificance in the then politics. However, their commercial importance can not be undermined and it was a must for the medieval commercial networks.

Such were the conditions prevailing in central Asia under the Mongols, which gave way to the rise of the globalization of its time. Silk-route was revived, having main centres of trade and commerce along it and in the periphery small cities and market connecting distant parts of the known world. Different communities indulging in trading activities had their offices and agents throughout the Asian and European kingdoms enjoying the protection under their Mongol patrons.

References

1. Joginder K. Chawla, *India's Overland Trade with Central Asia and Persia During the Thirteenth and Fourteenth Centuries* (New Delhi, 2006) , p. 10
2. Thomas T. Allsen, *Culture and Conquest in Mongol Eurasia*, (Cambridge University Press) , 2001, p. 10
3. See *The New Encyclopedia Britannica*, vol. 28 (1997), p. 234. The author of the article has a narrow approach. In fact the Chinese skill was required in the whole known civilized world not the Europe and Middle East alone. India, Persia and Iraq were also the ready takers of this knowledge.
4. *Cambridge History of Iran*, V. p. 222.

5. *Tarikh-i-Tabaristan*, p. 34.
6. *Cambridge History of Iran*, V, p. 142 and *The Lands of the Eastern Caliphate*, p. 408.
7. *History of the World Conqueror*, p. 77.
8. Howorth, I, p. 111.
9. Ibid, introduction, p. x.
10. *History of the World Conqueror*, p. 78.
11. *The Mongols and Russia*, pp. 127-28.
12. *Tabaqat-I-Nasiri*, p. 666 and *History of the World Conqueror*, p. 79. Hamadullah Mustawfi also speaks about the increased commercial relations between Persia and Mongolia and mentions the treacherous murder of the merchants by the governor of Utrar. He is the same chronicler who condemns the disaster and calamity brought by the Mongols in Persia in there worlds, "They came, they slew, they departed and deported". See *Tarikh-i-Guzida*, pp. 140-41.
13. Juvaini informs that the governor was one Inalchuq who was given the title of Khan. Among the merchant there was one Indian who addressed the governor simply as Inalchuq. On this account he became annoyed and embarrassed; at the same time he conceived a desire for their property, hence this event. See *History of the World Conqueror*, pp. 79-80, 367; *Tabaqat-i-Nasiri*, p. 967 and *Tarikh-i-Guzida*, pp. 140-41.
14. *Tabaqat-i-Nasiri*, p. 1041.
15. Ibid., p. 790
16. *Tabaqat-i-Nasiri*, pp. 1197-1202.
17. *Jamiut Tawarikh*, p. 76.
18. *Turks, Mongols and Others*, p. 62 n.270.
19. *Turkestan Down to the Mongol Invasions*, p. 464-65.
20. *Secret History of the Mongols*, p.
21. *Jamiut Tawarikh*, p. 80.
22. Ibid., p. 82.
23. Ibid., pp. 82-83.
24. *History of the World Conqueror*, pp. 603-604 and *Jamiut Tawarikh*, pp. 236-37.
25. Polo, ii, pp. 424-425.
26. *ibid*, p. 84.
27. Howorth, i, p. 159. Ata Malik Juwaini served as the governor of Baghdad. He abolished the imposts that had been levied in the countries of Tustar and Bayat, both in Khuzistan. See *History of the World Conqueror*, p. 34, nn. 23 and 24 for the location of these regions.
28. *Four Studies*, ii, p. 4.
29. Polo, ii, p. 478, n. 2 and Howorth, iii, p. 493.
30. *Cambridge History of Iran*, v, p. 542. Also see Rashiduddin Fazllullah, *Mukatibat-i-Rashidi*, edited by Muhammed Shafih (Lahore, 1947), letter No. 13 (p. 33) about the abolition of *tamgha* in Isfahan, letter No. 51

(pp. 122-23) about the complete abolition in various cities as quoted in G.D. Gulati, *North-west Frontier. . . .*, p. 98 and n. 6.

31. Ibid., p. 495; Percy Sykes, *A History of Persia,* third edition (London, 1969), pp. 113-14. Howorth, iii, pp. 525-27.
32. *Nuzhat-ul-Qulub,* pp. 164-66.
33. Howorth, iii, p. 632.
34. *History of the World Conqueror,* pp. 597 and notes 153 and 154. Also see pp. 97, 107-8, 215 and 218.
35. *The Mongol and Russia,* p. 390 and Michael Prawdin, p. 364.
36. Guilford A. Dudley, *A History of the Eastern Civilization,* p. 257.
37. One of the chief branches of the silk roads traversed western China, then followed the Oasis route (Khotan, Kashghar, Samarqand, Bukhara, Merv) across southern Central Asia into northern Persia and then westward to the Black Sea or the Mediterranean sea. *The New Encylopaedia Britannica,* Micropaedia, x (1977), p. 208. Also see *Cambridge Economic History of Europe,* ii, p. 34 about the limitless possibilities open to the western merchants by the Mongolian unification of Asia.
38. *Four Studies,* II, p. 1; K.A. Nizami, *Some Aspects of Religion and Politics,* P. 334. Contrary to the Mongols the conditions of the merchants in Europe was miserable as pointed out by Henri Pirrene. He writes that in Europe everywhere the foreigner was subject to special taxes, and unless he was protected by treaties, his goods ran a great risk of being requestioned by the territorial prince in case of need. Down to the end of the middle ages and even later, there existed a fair number of knights and barons who were the terror to merchants. See *Economic and Social History of Medieval Europe,* p. 93.
39. Scott C. Levi, *The Indian Diaspora in Central Asia and its Trade,* p. 91 and n. 15.
40. *Al Muqaddimah,* Eng. Tr. Rosenthal, ii, p. 309 and *The Encyclopedia of Islam,* new edition, x, p. 469.
41. Prior to the rise of the Mongols certain Turkish tribes have been found joining the caravans with the Arabs, Karluks and Tibetans to escape the turbulent tribes and the Uighurs in China. See E.H. Parker, *A Thousand Years of the Tartars,* p. 190
42. Ross E. Dunn, p. 67.
43. Burnes, ii, pp. 17-18. Thomas Witlam Atkinson also experienced a sandstorm extending four miles in width, and if traveler or a caravan were caught in them, the consequences were often fatal to man and beast. See his Travels in the regions of the upper and Lower Amoor and the Russian Acquisitions (London, 1860), pp. 295-96. Comparable with the account of caravan life in the first quarter of the twentieth century given by a Swedish geographer Sven Hedin in *The Silk Road,* pp. 48-50.

44. *The Encyclopedia Britannica,* iv, p. 861. Ibn Battuta and his party stayed in a hospice in Qunduz area for forty days in order to pasture their camels and horses and also for the fear of snow. See H.AR. Gibb, iii, pp. 586.
45. Peters, F.E. *The Hajj* (Delhi, 1996) , pp. 75-76. Soldier, traveler, writer and diplomat in the East India Company's Service, Sir Alexander Burnes left a beautiful account of his *Travels into Bokhara* published in three volumes. At one place he was moved by the fellow feeling in caravan and he writes, "In the society of a caravan, there is much good fellowship and many valuable lessons for a selfish man. It levels all distinctions between master and servant; and where both share every thing, it is impossible to be singular. Our servants now ate from the same dishes as ourselves. An Asiatic will never take a piece of bread, without offering a portion of it to those near him." (i, p. 252) At another place he wrote, "there was no disparting about the arrangement or order of the march (of the caravan) ; and it is a point of honour, that one shall at times wait for the other. If a single camel threw its load, the whole line halts till it is replaced; and one feels pleased at such universal sympathy. These feelings make it agreeable to travel in a caravan, for the detentions are much fewer than would really be imagined. The more I mingled with Asiatic in their own sphere, and judged them by their own standards. I imbibed more favourable impressions regarding them. One does not see in civilized Europe that generous feeling, which induces the natives of Asia, great and small, to share with each other every mouthful that they possess. Among Mahommedans we have no distinction of gentlemen and villain—at least, so far as hospitality in concerned. The khan fares as simply as the peasant; and never offers to raise a morsel to his lips till he has shared it with those near him. . . ." (ii, p. 20) .
46. H.A.R. Gibb, I, p. 249-50.
47. H.H. Howorth, iv, p. 39.
48. H.A.R.Gibb, i, p. 252. Marco Polo also speaks about the robbers and informs, "Yet, for all that the government can do, these brigands are not to be deterred from frequent depredations. Unless the merchants are well armed and equipped with bows, they stay and harry them unsparingly". See Polo, p. 31.
49. H.A.R.Gibb, iii, p. 591.
50. Ibid., i, pp. 160-63.
51. *The Encyclopedia Britannica,* iv, pp. 861-62 and *The New Encyclopedia Britannica,* ii, p. 844. For more details on Saljuq *Khans, Khans* of Syria, Mamluk *Khans* of Egypt and Syria and the *Khans* of the pilgrim route, the Ilkhanid and Safarid *Khans* of Iran and the *Khans* of Asia Minor see *The Encyclopedia of Islam,* New Edition, iv, pp. 1010-17.
52. *The Encyclopedia Britannica,* iv, pp. 861-862 and *The New Encyclopedia*

Britannica, ii, p. 844. HA.R. Gibb, I, pp. 160-163. Also see *Cambridge History of Islam*, ii, pp. 712-13, 717, 719 and 734.

53. *Hudud al Alam*, pp. 85, 87-88, 92, 97-99, 102, 107-8, 110-12, 118-19, 121-25, 127-28, 131-35, 137, 142, 153, 163. Chinese traveler of the medieval period witnessed caravansarais in Turkestan with doors and windows provided with glass. See *Medieval Researches*, I, pp. 130-31.
54. Al-Muqaddassi, p. 244.
55. *Cambridge History of Iran*, v, p. 86. Several numbers of buildings were discovered by various Russian expeditions, which have been identified as big caravanserais. Seen as a group they are quite striking by the variety of their internal arrangement; one of them seems even to have been covered with seventy-seven cupolas. The most spectacular among them is the celebrated Ribat-i-Malik whose date appeared to be secure around 1068-70 AD. The building belongs to our period by its impressive use of baked bricks, which articulate the outer walls in a manner reminiscent of pre-Islamic Soghdian architecture and by its impressive façade. Of greater interest for the history of cities are the urban caravanserais excavated at Siraf and published only in 1972. See *Cambridge History of Iran*, iv, pp. 346-48.
56. Ibid., p. 101.
57. Ibid., p. 277.
58. *The Lands of the Eastern Caliphate*, pp. 463-65.
59. *Cambridge History of Iran*, v, p. 511.
60. Ibid., p. 641.
61. *The Cambridge Economic History of Europe*, ii, p. 455.
62. Stanley Lane-Poole, *The Story of Cairo*, p. 270; Ross E. Dunn, p. 46 and Joginder K. Chawla, *India's Overland Trade*. p. 126.
63. Chawla op.cit., 126 and Sven Hedin, *Overland to India*, p. 22.
64. *Cambridge History of Iran*, vi, p. 419.
65. Halil Inalcik with Donald Quotaert (Ed.) *An Economic and Social History of the Ottoman Empire*: 1300-1914 (Cambridge 1994) , p. 196.
66. Ibid., p. 89.
67. Al-Muqaddassi, p. 249.
68. Ibid., p. 258.
69. Yule, I, p. 412.
70. Yule, II, pp. 191-92.
71. Gibb, iii, pp. 542-43. Shaikh Najm al-Din al-Kubra was one of the major saints of the Suhrawardi order, killed in the Mongols' capture of Gurganj in AD. 1221 (p. 542 n. 16). It is said that Chinghiz Khan, before sending his hordes against the city, dispatched a message to the celebrated Khwarizmi saint, the Sheikh Najm al-Din, the Kubra, advising him to leave the place, since the upshot might be its plunder and the slaughter of the people, but the Sheikh refused saying: "For eighty years have I dwelt here in its prosperity and should not leave it in the

day of its misfortune. I will take my chance with others, await my fate, whatever it may be and not fly from the Almighty's decree". He perished with the rest. See *Tabakat-i-Nasiri*, p. 1100n.

72. Ibid., ii, pp. 546-47.
73. Ibid., p. 554.
74. *History of the World Conqueror,* p. 552-53. Shaykh Sayf al-Din Bakharzi had been a disciple of Najmal-Din Kubra in Urganj, the founder of the Kubraviya order of dervishes, who at a critical moment sent him with a proselytizing mission to Bukhara. While Kubra perished during the storming of Urganj by the Mongols. Bakhazi not only survived their seizure of Bukhara but also subsequently attained such prestige that Berka Khan of Golden Horde came to Bukhara to visit the shaykh. Sorqaqtani, the widow of Tolu and mother of Great Khan Monke and Qubilay, herself a Christian, is said to have donated the considerable sum of 1000 *balish* of silver for a madrassa to be built and maintained in Bukhara and gave instructions that Sayf al-Din Bakharzi become the *mudabbir* (principal) of the school *mutavalli* (administrator) of the *waqf* endowment. See Svat Soucek, *A History of Inner Asia* (Cambridge, 2000), pp. 117-18.
75. Gibb, ii, p. 555 and n. 59.
76. Ibid., pp. 568-69.
77. Ibid., p. 570.
78. Here Ibn Battuta tells us an anecdote about this hospice that how that woman got it built by selling her garment, embroidered with jewels of great value. Because the robe was shown to the Caliph who had lighted the eye on it, therefore she ordered the robe to be sold and built with its price the above structure. After the building was completed there remained of the (price of the) robe as much as one third which she ordered it to be buried under one of the columns of the mosque that it might be available and come to light if needed in future. This tradition was related to Chinghiz Khan who ordered in consequence to pull down the columns in this mosque. After about a third had been pulled down without finding anything he left the rest as they were. See *ibid,* pp. 572-73.
79. Ibid., pp. 573-74.
80. Ibid., pp. 580-81.
81. Ibid., pp. 582-83.
82. Ibid., pp. 583-84.
83. Ibid., pp. 585.
84. Ibid., pp. 585-86 and note 185.
85. Ibid., pp. 586-87 and note 192.
86. Ibid., pp. 589-90.
87. Ibid., pp. 590-91.
88. Ibid., pp. 591-52.

89. *Hudud al-Alam*, pp. 38-39 and 113. Al Muqaddassi (p. 248) gives a brief accout of Samarqand which was the capital of al-Sughd, the metropolis of the rigion-a splendial, important ancient town, a brilliant and elegant metropolis; comfortable, in the numerous slaves, abundent water from a deep river; buildings were storng, high and solid. The mode of life was pleasant, routes led to it, commodities were carried thether from distance places. The science floushed there, and the learned man was honoured. Here was an aboundance of horses, men, and wealth. Residents and merchants met there. In summer it was paradeise. . .
90. *Lata if al-ma' arif*, p. 140. About the origin of the paper manufacturing at Samarkand, Alberuni also gives us resembling account. He relates the same story that Chinese prisoners at Samarkand introduced the fabrication of paper and there upon it was made at various places so as to meet the existing demand of that period. See Alberuni, *India*, p. 171 and *Turkestan Down to the Mongol Invasions*, pp. 236-37.
91. Al-Idrisi, p. 52.
92. *History of the World Conqueror*, p. 122.
93. *Medieval Researches*, I, pp. 21-22 and notes 29-33.
94. ibid, pp. 76-78 and notes 194-199. At another place we find a reference of gardens and groves and the Chinese gardens, which according to the traveler could not be compared with those of Samarqand. See p. 81 and note 205.
95. Among other medicinal plants Chang Te tells about *a-si-rh*, which, was useful in cases of relained placenta. It was also employed in wounds inflicted by sharp weapons when the pus was not discharged. The *nu-ko-sa-rh* was also useful curing wounds inflicted by sharp weapons, ruptures of bowels and of the tendons. By rubbing this medicine, after it and been masticated, into the affected parts the divided portions drew together. It was not possible to enumerate all the drugs as pointed out by the author. See *Medieval Researches*, I, pp, 131-32.
96. *Tabakat-i-Nasiri*, pp. 122-23.
97. Polo, i, p. 183.
98. He gives the names of different tombs in the city and further writes "On the outskirts of Samarqand is a tomb which is called Dasht Qatawan and Yakut concerning this states the Prophet said—*Beyond Samarqand is a village that is called Qatawin; from here 70,000 martyrs will go forth, each of whom will make intercession for 70,000 of the members of his Kith and kin.* Now since this country in those former times was in the land of the Infidels, people wondered much as to the true meaning of this Tradition. Until at length, in the days of Sultan Sanjar the Saljuq, a battle took place at this spot between the army of Islam and the Infidels of the Qara Khitay, when a great multitude of Moslems was martyred; and then again during the irruption of the Mongols an equally great

multitude of the people of Islam attained here to the rank of martyrdom: whereby men were enlightened as to the true meaning of the Tradition. See *Nuzhat al-Qulub*, pp. 237-238.

99. Ibid., p. 193.
100. Polo, p. 291 note. Yule while giving extract from the historical *Encyclopedia of Rashiduddin* gives the name of the city as Semali, most of the inhabitant of which were natives of Samarqand. See Yule, *Cathay and the Way Thither*, iii, p. 117.
101. See G.D. Gulati, "Ibn Battuta in Transoxiana" published in the *Proceedings of the Indian History Congress*, 58th session, Bangalore, 1997, pp. 772-78. Also see Chawla, op.cit,, pp. 52-53.
102. *The Lands of the Eastern Caliphate*, pp. 463-65.
103. *Tamerlane*, p. 17
104. Chawla, op. cit., p. 53 and *Cambridge History of Iran*, v, pp. 414-15.
105. *Baburnamah*, pp. 74-77 and 81 and Thakstan, 82-84.
106. *Hudud al-Alam*, p. 112.
107. *The Lands of the Eastern Caliphate*, pp. 461-63; *Encyclopedia of Islam*, ii, p. 778. For brief account of the city and its various gates see Chawla op. cit, p. 54.
108. See Scott C. Levi, *The Indian Diaspora in Central Asia and its Trade*, 1550-1900, p. 91.
109. *Medieval Researches*, i, p. 22
110. Gibb, iii, pp. 550-51. As already noted above, Ibn Battuta lodged in Bukhara in its suburb called Fath Abad and he describes in details the hospice of Shaikh Saifal-Din-Bakharzi.
111. *Nuzhat-Al-Qulub*, pp. 193-94, 196 and 198-99,
112. ibid, pp. 254-55.
113. Scott C. Levi, p. 91.
114. *Baburnamah*, pp. 82-83 and Thackston, p. 87.
115. Arminis Vambery, *History of Bukhara*, Introduction, p. 25.
116. For details see *Turkestan Down to the Mongol Invasions*, p. 16.
117. Ibid., pp. 134-35. At another place he writes that there can be no doubt that before the Mongol invasion, for unknown reasons, Kish and its neighbourhood fell into decay and Nasaf began to flourish in its stead (p. 427) . Minhaj speaks of Kish as the capital of the Sea of Fars. See *Tabakat-i-Nasiri*, I, 179 and note 4.
118. *Hudud al-Atam*, p. 113. *Chu-fan-chi*, pp. 133-34 and see Al muqaddasi, p. 251. W. Barthold on the basis of the account of Ibn al-Athir also mentions Kish island as a port. He writes that at the beginning of thirteenth century the overland trade with China was of still greater importance than formerly, as the sea trade was rendered precarious by the accident of a dispute between the two rulers of two ports of in the Persian Gulf, Ormuz and Kish, each of whom in every possible way prevented merchants from setting out from the post belonging to the

other. See *Turkestan Down to the Mongol Invasions,* p. 395.
119. *History of the World Conqueror,* p. 521.
120. *The Lands of the Eastern Caliphate,* p. 470.
121. *Nuzhat al-Qulub,* p. 254.
122. *Baburnama,* pp. 83-84.
123. *The Encyclopedia of Islam,* New Edition, vi, p. 618.
124. *Hudud-al-Alam,* p. 105.
125. *Medieval Researches,* pp. 103-4.
126. Al Muqaddisi, pp. 263-64 and 273 see also *The Encyclopedia of Islam,* vi, p. 618.
127. *Lata if al-maarif,* p. 135 and the *Encyclopedia of Islam,* vi, p. 618.
128. *The Encyclopedia of Islam,* vi, pp. 618-20.
129. *History of the World Conqueror,* p. 153.
130. ibid, pp. 161-64.
131. *Nuzhat al Qulub,* p. 34.
132. Ibid., p 251
133. *Hudud al-Alam,* pp. 85-86
134. *Medieval Researches,* pp. 47-49.
135. Polo, p. 51.
136. Ibid., p. 50.
137. Ibid., p. 51

7

Conclusion

It is the geo-polity of Central Asia which has played a vital role in its history. The rise of the Mongols under Chinghiz Khan in the beginning of the thirteenth century changed the whole map of Asia and Europe. New kingdoms were formed after the death of this great warrior who not only followed his *yasa* but also took the task of rebuilding of the ruined cities throughout the Asiatic lands where they had controlled different routes and passages. These kingdoms remained independent with acknowledging the superiority of the Yuans in China. But the Chaghatai Khanate jointly governed by the successors of Chaghatai and Qaidu, defied the superiority of the Yuan Qaan and rather challenged their rule in their homeland for a longer period till they were subjugated.

Chaghatai Khanate did not maintain peace with the Ilkhans of Persia and sometimes had differences with the Khans of the Golden Horde in Russia also. The balance of power mostly remained in the hands of the Chaghadaids. They became powerful and controlled the whole chain of routes connecting India with Central Asia. Specially after taking possession of Kabul and Ghazni, line of control on the north-west frontier of India became the integral part of their empire. Hence began the unbroken series of campaign into Hindustan. The Sultans of Delhi through their punitive steps against the Mongol invasions were successful to save the Sultanate. Alauddin Khalji revolutionarised his economy in the light of the recurring Mongol inroads. In Central Asia drastic changes took place after the death of Dava Khan and it paved the way for the rise of the Turks soon and the whole empire was cut into pieces which later gave way to the Barlas Turks to unite once again the whole region under Timur.

The contribution of the Mongols in Central Asia is unique in its commercial network. These were the Mongols who unified Asia and Europe while controlling the Asian trade-routes through which passed, the caravans of the medieval merchants. The narratives of the journeys of medieval travellers such as Marco Polo, Carpini and other Europeans and Ibn Battuta are the best example of the peace and security prevailing in the Mongol Kingdoms. They did their best to provide all facilities apart from maintaining the safety and security on the roads, introducing the *yams* (Horse-post-stations) throughout the empire. The attitude of the Mongol towards trading-communities was an example of the encouragement and support they afforded for the commercial networks to function smoothly and profitably.

Traveling those days was not without risk. The hazards of wild animal, tribes, weather, robbers and long deserts were a common features. Undoubtedly traveling in the caravans was considered a more conducive and safe. Organized caravans and construction of caravansarais, *ribatats* or sarais and sufi *khanqahs* were the salient features of the medieval long-distance trade. Traders from all over the known world, thronged together in the cities, markets and towns of Central Asia and other kingdoms. Number of foreign settlements could be witnessed while engaged in their business. Exchange of goods from distant lands of Asia and Europe had resulted in bringing prosperity for the merchants as well as for their Mongol patrons. The Mongol nomads soon tasted the benefits of the settled life of the towns and ultimately preferred to follow urbanized pattern of living. The disintegration of the Mongols gave way to ruling agents of Central Asia and emergence of new empires in the coming days. The best examples are the Uzbeks, Mughals and the Ottomans.

Bibliography

PRIMARY SOURCES

Afif, Shama Siraj, *Tarikh-i-Firuzshahi*, Hindi translation by S.A.A. Rizvi and English Translation by R C Jauhri, Delhi, 2002.

Ahmed, Nizamuddin, *Tabaqat-i-Akbari*, English translation by B.De, volume I, Reprint Calcutta, 1973.

Alberuni, *Alberuni's India*, English Translation E. Sachau, popular edition, Delhi 1954.

Al-Biruni, *India*, Abridged edition of E.C. Sachau's English translation, edited by Qeyamuddin Ahmad, New Delhi, 1995.

Anonymous. *Hudud al Alam*, English translation by V. Minorsky, Oxford, 1937.

Attar, Farid al-Din, *The Ilahi-Nama*, translation into English by J.A. Boyhe, Manchester, 1976.

Babur, Zahiruddin Muhammad, *Baburnama*, English translation by A.S. Beveridge, Indian reprint, New Delhi, 1979.

Badaoni, Abdul Qadir, *Muntkhab-ut-Tawarikh*, English translation by S.A. Ranking in 3 vols., Patna, 1973.

Barani, Ziauddin, *Tarikh-i-Firuzshahi*, Hindi translation by S.A.A. Rizvi and English extracts by Elliot and Dowson. *Fatwa i Jahandari*, Hindi translation by S.A.A. Rizvi.

Batutta Ibn, *The Travels of Ibn Battuta* English Translation by H.A.R. Gibb in 3 vols, First Indian edition, New Delhi, 1993.

— *The Rehla of Ibn Battuta* (India, Maldive Islands and Ceylon) Translation and commentary by Mahdi Hussain, Baroda, 1976.

Bhakhari, Sayyid Muhammad Masumi, *Tarikh-i-Sind*, Hindi Translation by S.A.A. Rizvi.

Bhandari, Sujan Rai, *Khulasat-ut-Tawarikh*, Punjabi translation by Punabi Unviersity, Patiala, 1970.

Chau Ju-Kua, *Chu-fan-Chi*, English translation by Freidrich Hirth and W.W. Rockhill, New York, 1966.

Chun, Chang, *The Travels of an al Chemist* recorded by Li Chih Chang and translated by Arthur Walley, London, 1931.

Dehlawi, Amir Hasan Al Sijzi, *Fawaid al Fuad*, English Translation by Zia-ul-Hasan Faruqi, New Delhi, 1996.

Dughlat, Mirza Muhammad Haidar, *Tarikh-i-Rashidi*, English translation by E. Denison Ross, Indian edition, Patna, 1972.

Fazl, Abul, *Ain-I-Akbari*, volume II, English transaltion by H.S. Jarrett, third edition, New Delhi, 1978.

Fazlullah, Rashiduddin, *Jami-ut-Twarikh*, English translation by J.A. Boyle under the title of *The Successors of Chingiz Khan*, London, 1971.

Ferishta, Mahomed Kasim, *Tarikh-i-Ferishta*, English translation by John Briggs under the title, *Rise of Mahomedan Power in India*, vol. I, First reprint, Delhi, 1990.

Firuzeshah, *Futuhat-i-Firuzeshahi*, Hindi Translation by S.A.A. Rizvi.

Grigor of Akane, *History of the Nation of the Archers*, [The Mongols], The Armenian text, edited with an English translation and Notes by Robert P. Blake and Richard N. Frye, Cambridge, 1954.

Hazi Ad-Dabir, Abdullah Muhammad Al Makki Al Asaf Al Ulughkhani, *Zafar ul wali bi Muzaffar wa Alihi*, English transaltion by M.F. Lokhandawala under the title of *An Arabic History of Gujrat*, vol. II, Baroda, 1974.

Idrisi, Al-Sharif, *Kitab Nuzhat al Mushtaq,* English Translation with commentary S. Maqbul Ahmad, Leiden, 1960.

Isami, *Futuhus Salatin* English translation by Agha Mahdi Hussain, Volume II, 1978.

Isfandiyar, Muhammad bin al Hasan bin, *History of Tabaristan,* an abridged English Translation by Edward G. Browne, London, 1905.

Juvaini, Ata Malik, *Tarikh-i-Jahan-I-Gusha,* English translation by J.A. Boyle under the title *History of the World Conqueror,* Manchester, University Press, 1958. Second edition with a new introduction and bibliography by David O. Morgan under the title *Genghis Khan: The History of the World Conqueror,* Manchester University Press, 1997.

Khaldun, Ibn, *al Muqaddimah,* English translation by Franz Rosenthal as *The Muqaddima: An Introduction to History,* 3 vols., New York, 1958.

Khusrau, Amir, *Qiranussadain, Khazaninul Futuh, Miftahul Futuh, Nuh Sipihr, and Tughluquamah,* Hindi translation by S.A.A.Rizvi.

Kufi, Ali bin Hamid bin Abi Bakr, *Chachnama,* English translation by Mirza Kalichbeg, Fredunbeg, reprint, Delhi, 1979.

Major, R.H., *India in the Fifteenth Century,* Indian reprint, Madras, 1942.

Siraj, Minhajuddin, *Tabakat-i-Nasiri,* English translation by H.G. Raverty in 2 vols. Reprint, Calcutta, 1995.

Mudabbir, Fakhr-i-, *Aadabul Harb Washjuat,* Hindi translation S.A.A. Rizvi.

Multani, Ainulmulk, *Inshi-i-Mahru,* partly Hindi translation by S.A.A. Rizvi.

Muqaddasi, Al-, *Ahsan al-Tqasin fi Marifat al-Aqalim,* English translation by Basil Anthony Collins and reviewed by Muhammad Hamid Al-Tai under the title, *The Best Division For Knowledge of the Regions,* South Street, *U.K.,* 1994

Mushtaqi, Rizqullah, *Waqiat-i-Mushtaqi,* English translation by I.H. Siddiqui, New Delhi, 1992 and Hindi translation by S.A.A. Rizvi.

Mustawfi, Hamdulah, *Nuzhat al Qulub,* English translation by G.Le Strange, London, 1919.

—, *Tarikh-i-Guzida,* English translation by Edward G. Browne, London, 1913.

Nizami, Tajuddin Hasan, *Tajul Maathir,* English Translation by Bhagwat Saroop, Delhi, 1998 and Hindi translation by S.A.A. Rizvi.

Pelsaert, Francisco, *Jahangir's India,* English translation by W.H. Moreland and P. Geyl, Cambridge, 1925.

Polo, Marco, *The Book of Ser Marco Polo,* English translation by Sir Henry Yule in 2 vols., London, 1929 and *The Travels of Marco Polo:* by Ronald Latham, Baltimore, 1958.

Qalqashandi, *Subh ul Asha,* English Translated by O. Spies, entitled, *An Arab Account of India in the fourteenth Century,* being translation of the chapters on India, Aligarh, 1941 and by M,.A.A. Zaki in *Arab Accounts of India,* Delhi, 1981.

Sirhindi, Yahya bin Ahmed bin Abdullah, *Tarikh-i-Mubarakshahi,* English Translation by K.K. Basu, Baroda, 1932.

Sulayman al Tajir, *Akhbar Al Sin wa'L-Hind,* English translation by S. Maqbul Ahmad under the title, *Arabic Classical Accounts of India and China,* Simla, 1989.

Sun, Kei Kwei, *The Secret History of the Mongol Dynasty,* Tr. And & Edited with Introduction and Notes, Aligarh, 1957.

Timur, *Institutes,* English translation by Maor Davy, Oxford, 1783.

Umari Al-, *Masalik al-Absar fi Mamalik al-Amsar,* English translation by Muhammad Zaki under the title *Arab Accounts of India,* Delhi, 1981.

Vladimirtsov, B.Ya., *The Life of Chingis-Khan,* Tr. From Russian by Prince D.S. Misky, London, 1930.

Yazdi, Maulana Sharfuddin Ali, *Zafarnamah,* Hindi translation S.A.A. Rizvi.

MODERN WORKS

Abdullah, Ahmad, *The Historical Background of Pakistan,* Karachi, 1973.

Abraham, Meera, *Two Medieval Merchant Guilds of South India,* Delhi, 1988.

Aggarwal, R.S. *Trade Centres and Routes in Northern India,* Delhi, 1982.

Adshead, S.A.M., *Central Asia in World History,* London, 1993.

Ahmad, Aziz, *Studies in Islamic Culture in the Indian Environment,* Oxford, 1964.

—, *Political History and Institution of the Early Turkish Empire of Delhi,* Delhi, 1972.

Ahmad, Kazi. S.A. *Georgraphy of Pakistan,* second edition, Karachi, 1966.

Ahmad, S. Maqbul, *Indo-Arab Relations,* New Delhi, 1967.

Ahmad S. Maqbul and A. Rahman, *Al-Masudi, Millenary Commemoration Volume,* Aligarh, 1960.

Allsen, Thomas T., *Culture and Conquest in Mongol Eurasia,* Cambridge, 2001

—, *Commodity and Exchange in the Mongol Empire: A Cultural History of Islamic Textiles,* Cambridge, 1997.

Amitai-Preiss, Reuven and David O. Morgan, *The Mongol Empire and its Legacy,* Leiden, 1999.

Amitai Reuven and Michaal Biran (Ed.), *Mongols, Turks and Others: Eurasian Nomads and the Sedentary World,* Leiden, Brill, 2005.

Arabshah, Ahmed Ibn, *Tamerlane or Timur The Great Amir,* English Translation by J.H. Saunders from the Arabic text, First Reprint, Lahore, 1976.

Ashraf, K.M. *Life and Conditions of the People of Hindustan,*

Second edition, New Delhi, 1970.

Ashtor, E.A. *Social and Economic History of the Near East in the Middle Ages*, London, 1976.

Asimov, M.S. and C.E. Bosworth, *History of Civilizations of Central Asia, Vol. IV, The Age of Achievement: A.D. 750 to the end of the fifteenth century, Part One, The Historical Social and Economic Setting*, First Indian Edition, Delhi 1999.

Askari, S.H., *Amir Khusrau as a Historian*, Patna, 1992.

—, On Awfi's *Jawami-ul-Hikayat*, Patna, 1995.

Atkinson, Thomas Witlam, *Travels in the Regions of Upper and Lower Amoor and the Russian Acquisitions*, London, 1860.

Baqir, Muhammed, *Lahore: Past and Present*, reprint, Delhi, 1984.

Barthold, V.V., *Four Studies on the History of Central Asia*, Vol. I, Leiden, 1956, vol. II, Leiden, 1958.

Barthold, W., *Turkestan Down to the Mongol Invasion*, First Indian edition, New Delhi, 1992.

Bayly, C.A., *Rulers, Townsmen and Bazaars: North Indian Society in the Age of British Expansion*, 1770-1879, Cambridge, 1983.

Beazley, C.R., *The Dawn of Modern Geography* in 3 vols., New Delhi, 1949.

Becker, Jasper, *The Lost Country: Mongolia Revealed*, London, 1992.

Biran, Michal, *Qaidu and the Rise of the Independent State in Central Asia*, Survey, 1997.

Bold, Bat-Ochir, *Mongolian Nomadic Society: A Reconstructions of the 'Medieval' History of Mongolia*, Curzon, Survey, 2001.

Blunt, Wilfrid, *The Golden Road to Samarkand*, London, 1973.

Bosworth, C.E. *The Ghaznavides*, Edinburgh, 1963.

Boyle, J.A. [Ed.] *Cambridge History of Iran*, vol. V, Cambridge, 1968.

—, Persia: *History and Heritage*, London, 1978.

Brent, Peter, *The Mongol Empire*, London, 1976.

Brestschneider E. *Medieval Researches* in 2 vols, London, 1887.

Burnes, Alexander, *Travels into Bokhara,* London, Karachi, 1973 (1834) 3 vils.

Chambers, James, *The Devil's Horsemen: The Mongol Invasion of Europe,* 1988.

Chattopadhyaya, B.D., *The Making of Early Medieval India,* Delhi, 1984.

Chawla, Joginder K., *India's Overland Trade with Central Asia and Persia During the Thirteenth and Fourteenth Centuries,* New Delhi, 2006.

Christian, David, *A History of Russia, Central Asia and Mongolia,* Volume I *Inner Eurasian from Pre-history to the Mongol Empire,* Oxford, 1998.

Cook, M.A. [Ed.] *Studies in the Economic History of the Middle East,* London, 1970.

Curtin, J. *The Mongols,* London, a reprint of 1908.

Curtin, Philip D., *Cross-cultural Trade in World History,* Cambridge, 1984.

Davar, Firoze Cowasji, *Iran and India through the Ages,* Bombay, 1962.

Davies, C.C. *An Historical Atlas of the Indian Peninsula,* Oxford, 1949.

Day, U.N., *Some Aspects of Medieval India,* Delhi, 1972.

—, *The Government of the Sulanate,* Delhi, 1972.

—, *Medieval Malwa,* Delhi, 1965.

Dichter, David. *The North-West Frontier of West Pakistan: A Study in Regional Geography,* Oxford, 1967.

Dudley, Guilford, A., *A History of Eastern Civilization,* London, 1937.

Douie, Sir James. *The Punjab, North-West Frontier Province and Kashmir,* Cambridge, 1916.

Dunn, Ross, E. *The Adventures of Ibn Battuta,* London, 1986.

Dupree, Louis, *Afghanistan,* Princeton, 1973.

Elliot and Dowson, *History of India as told by its own Historians* in 8 vols., Allahabad, 1972.

Elphinstone, Mountstuart, *An Account of the Kingdom of Cabul,* in 2 volumes, reprinted, Karachi, 1974.

Embree, Ainslie, T., *Pakistan's Western borderlands,* New Delhi.

— , (Ed.) *Encyclopaedia of Asian History,* Volume 3, London, 1988.

Fairlay, Jean, *The Lost River the Indus,* London, 1975.

Farmer, Edward L. and others, *Comparative History of Civilization in Asia,* volume I, U.S.A., 1977.

Farooqi, M.A., *The Economic Policy of the Delhi Sultans of India,* Delhi, 1991.

Farooque, Abul Khair Muhammad, *Roads and Communications in Mughal India,* Delhi, 1977.

Fisher, W.B. [Ed.] *Cambridge History of Iran,* vol. I, Cambridge, 1968.

Foltz, Richard C., *Religions of the Silk Road: Overland Trade and Cultural Exchange from Antiquity to the Fifteenth Century, London,* 1999.

Fox, Ralph, *Genghis Khan,* London, 1937.

Franke, Herbert and Denis Twitchett, [Ed.] *Cambridge History of China,* volume 6, *Alien regimes and border states,* 907-1368, Cambridge, 1994.

Fraser, James B., *Narratives of a Journey into Khorasan in the years 1821 and 1822,* Reprint, Delhi, 1984.

Frykenberg, R.E., *Delhi Through the Ages: Essays in Urban History, Culture and Society,* 1986.

Gafurov, B.G. *Central Asia: Pre-Historic to Pre-Modern Times* (Being the first English version of *Tazhiki* in Rusian), 2 volumes, Kolkata, 2005.

Gernet, Jackques, *Daily Life in China on the Eve of the Mongol Invasion 1250-1276,* Translated from the French by H.M. Wright, California, 1962.

—, *A History of Chinese Civilization,* Translated from the French by J.R. Foster, Cambridge, 1985.

Gibb, H.A.R. *The Arab Conquests in Central Asia,* London, 1923.

Goitein, S.D., *Studies in Islamic History and Institutions,* Leiden, 1968.

Gopal, Lallani, *The Economic Life of Northern India,* A.D. 700-A.D. 1200, Patna, 1965.

Gulati, G.D., *India's North-West Frontier in Pre-Mughal Times,* Delhi, 1985.

Habib, Irfan and T. Raychaudhuri, *Cambridge Economic History of India,* vol. I, Cambridge, 1982.

Habib, Mohammad and K.A. Nizami, *A Comprehensive History of India,* volume V, *Delhi Sultanate,* New Delhi, 1970.

Habibullah, A.B.M. *The Foundation of Muslim Rule in India,* second revised edition, Allahabad, 1961.

Hedin, Sven, *Overland Trade to India* in 2 volumes, first green and reprinting, New York, 1968.

The Silk Road, Translated from Swedish by F.H. Lyon, Delhi, 1994.

Hambly, Gavin and others [Ed.], *Central Asia,* London, 1969.

Hamilton, Walter, *Description of Hindustan and the Adjacent Countries,* 2 volumes, First Indian Reprint, Delhi, 1971.

Hartog, Leo de, *Genghis Khan: Conqueror of the World,* London, 1989.

Russia and the Mongol Yoke: The History of the Russian Principalities and the Golden Horde, London, 1996.

Herbert, Thomas, *Travels in Persia* [1627-29], abridged and edited by Sir William Foster, London, 1928.

Hildinger, Erik, *Warriors of the Steppes: A Military History of Central Asia,* 500 B.C., to 1700 A.D, U.S.A. 2001

Hilton, Richard, *Historical Atlas of Iran,* Tehran University, 1971.

Hodgson, Marshall G.S., *The Venture of Islam,* Lahore, 2004.

Hodivala, S.H. Studies in *Indo-Muslim History,* Bombay, 1939.

Holdich, Sir, T.H., *India,* first Indian reprint, New Delhi, 1975.

—, *The Indian Borderland,* London, 1909.

—, *The Gates of India*, London, 1910.

Holt, P.M. and others [Ed.] *The Cambridge History of Islam*, volume I, *The Central Islamic Lands*, volume II, The Further Islamic Lands: *Islami Society and Civilization*, Cambridge, 1970.

Hookham, Hilda, *Tamburlaine The Conqueror*, London, 1962.

Howorth, H.H. *History of the Mongols*:

—, Vol. I, London, 1876;

—, Vol. II, division II, London, 1880;

—, Vol. III, London, 1888;

—, Vol. IV, London, 1927.

Huntington, Ellseworth, *The Pulse of Asia: A Journey in Central Asia illustrating the geographical basis of history*, New York, 1907.

Husain, Agha Mahdi, *The Tughluq Dynasty*, Calcutta, 1963.

—, *Rise and Fall of Muhammad Bin Tughluq*, Reprint, Delhi, 1972.

Husain, Yusuf, *Glimpses of Medieval Indian Culture*, Bombay, 1957.

—, *Two Studies in Early Mughal History*, Simla, 1976.

Hutton, James, *Central Asia from the Aryan to the Cossack*, reprint of 1895 (2005).

Inalcik, Halil with Donald Quotaert (Ed.), *An Economic and Social History of the Ottoman Empire: 1300-1914*, Cambridge, 1994.

Ischbodlin, Boris, *Essays on Tatar History*, New Delhi, 1963.

Jackson Peter, *The Delhi Sultanate: A Political and Military History*, Cambridge, 1999.

Jain, L.C. *Indigenous Banking in India*, London, 1929.

Jain, P.C. *Socio-Economic Exploration of Medieval India* from 800 to 1300 A.D., Delhi, 1976.

Jain, V.K., *Trade and Traders in Western India* [A.D. 1000-1300], New Delhi, 1990.

Jagchid, Senhin and Paul Hyer, *Mongolia's Culture and Society*,

1979.

Juntunen, Mirja and Birgit N. Schlyter (ed.), *Return to Silk Routes: Current Scandinavian Research on Central Asia,* London, 1999.

Kaji, Dewan Bahadur, H.L., *Lands Beyond the Border,* second edition, Oxford, 1948.

Khan, Zafarul-Islam and Zaki, Yakub, *Hajj in Focus,* London, 1986.

Khazanov, A.M. *Xomads and the Outside World,* origionally in Russian (1983), translated into English by Julia Crookenden, Cambridge, 1984.

Khazanov, Anatoly M. and Andre Wink (Ed.), *Nomads in the Sedentary World, Curzon,* Survey, 2001.

Komatroff, Linda (ed.) *Beyond the Legacy of Genghis Khan,* E.J. Brill, Leidon, 2006.

Krader, Lawrence, *Peoples of Central Asia, Hague,* 1963.

Kwanten, Luc, *A History of Central Asia,* 500-1500, *Imperial Nomads* Leicester University Press, 1979.

Lal, K.S., *History of the Khaljis, Bombay,* 1967

—, *Growth of Muslim Population in Medieval India,* 1973.

—, *The Legacy of Muslim Rule in India,* New Delhi, 1992.

Lamb, Alastair, *Asian Frontiers: Studies in a Continuing Problem,* London, 1968.

Lamb, Harold, *The March of the Barbarians,* London, 1941.

Genghis Khan: The Conquoror Emperor of all Men, New York, a reprint of 1927 (1963).

Lambrick, *H.T. Sind : A general introduction,* Hyderabad, Sind, 1964.

Lane-Poole, *Stanley,*

—, *The Muhammadan Dynasties,* Republished, New York, 1965.

—, *The Story of Cairo,* London, 1902.

Lapidus, I.M., *Muslim Cities in the Later Middle Ages* [950-1350], Cambridge, 1976.

Larner, John, *Marco Polo and the Discovery of the World,* London,

1999.

Latif, S.M., *History of the Punjab,* New Delhi, 1974.

Lattimore, Owen, *Studies in Frontier History,* Oxford, 1962.

Levi, Scott C., *The Indian Diaspora in Central Asia and its Trade: 1550-1900,* Brill, 2001.

Lewis, Bernard, *Islam Religion and Society,* 1974.

—, *The World of Islam: Faith, People, Culture [Ed.]* London, Reprinted 1977.

Lane, George, *Genghis Khan and Mongol Rule,* Greenwood Press, London, 2004.

—, *Early Mongol Rule in Thirteenth Century Iran,* London, Routledge, Curzon, 2003.

Lister, R.P., *The Secret History of Genghis Khan,* London, 1969.

Lockhart, Lawrence, *Persian Cities,* London, 1960.

Malleson, G.B. *History of Afghanistan,* London, 1878.

Martin, H. Desmond, *The Rise of Chingiz Khan and his conquest of Northern China,* Baltimore, 1950.

Manz, Beatrice F., [Ed.] *Central Asia in Historical Perspective,* Oxford, 1994.

Marozzi, Justin, *Tamerlane,* London, 2004.

Masson, Charles, *Narrative of Various Journeys in Baluchistan, Afghanistan and the Punjab,* in 3 volumes, Karachi, 1974.

Mazumdar, B.P., *The Economic History of Northern India,* Calcutta, 1960.

Medieval India : A Miscellany, Centre of Advanced Study, Department of History, Aligarh Muslim University, Aligarh.

—, Vol. I, 1969;

—, Vol. II, 1972;

—, Vol. III, 1975;

—, Vol. IV, 1977.

Mirza, Mohammad Wahid, *The Life and Works of Amir Khusrau,* Delhi, 1974.

Mishra, S.C., *The Rise of Muslim Power in Gujrat,* Baroda, 1963.

Mishra, S.D. *Rivers of India,* New Delhi, 1970.

Morgan, David, *The Great Yasa of Chingiz Khan and Mongol Law in the Ilkhanete,* BSOAS, 49/1 (1986), pp. 163-176.

David, *Mongols,* Oxford, 1986.

Medieval Persia, London, 1988.

Moorcraft, Wiliam, *Travels in the Himalayan provinces of Hindustan and the Punjab, in Ladakh and Kashmir, in Peshawar, Kabul, Kunduz and Bokhara,* 2 volumes, reprinted, New Delhi, 1971.

Moreland, W. H., *The Agrarian System of Moslem India,* Allahabad, 1929.

Nadvi, Maulana Masud Ali Sahib, *Hindustan Arbon ki nazar mein,* Part II, Azamgarh, 1960, Part II, Azamgarh, 1962.

Naqvi, Hamida Khatoon, *Agricultural, Industrial and Urban Dynamism Under the Sultans of Delhi,* New Delhi, 1986.

Nazim, Muhammad, *The Life and Times of Sultan Mahmud,* second edition, New Delhi, 1971.

Needham, Joseph, *Science and Civilization in China,* Cambridge, 1971.

Newton, Arthur Percival, *Travel and Travellers of The Middle Ages,* revised, London, 1968.

Nigam, S.B.P., *Nobility under the Sultans of Delhi,* Delhi, 1968.

Niyogi, Pushpa, *Contributions to the Economic History of Northern India,* Calcutta, 1962.

Nizami, K.A., *Studies in Medieval Indian History and Culture,* Allahabad, *1966.*

—, *Some Aspects of Religion and Politics during the thirteenth century,* Delhi, *1974.*

—, *Politics and Society during the early Medieval Period, Vol. I,* Aligarh, *1974.*

—, *State and Culture in medieval India, new Delhi, 1985.*

—, *The Life and Times of Shaikh Farid-ul-Din Gunj-I-Shakar, Reprint,* Delhi, *1987.*

Oliver, Edwar E., *Across the Border,* London, 1890.

Pal, M.K., *Crafts and Craftsmen in Traditional India,* New Delhi,

1978.

Pandey, A.B., *The First Afghan Empire in India,* Calcutta, 1956,

Pearson, M.N., *Pious Passage: The Hajj in Earlier Times,* New Delhi, 1994.

Parker, E.H., *A Thousand Years of the Tartars,* London, 2002.

Peters, F.E,, *The Hajj,* Delhi, 1996.

Phillip, E.D. *Mongols,* London, 1969.

Phillip, Thomas and Ulrich Haarmann, *The Mamluks in Egyptian Politics and Society,* Cambridge, 1998.

Pirrene, Henri, *Economic and Social History of Medieval Europe,* London, 1936.

Postan, M.M., Rica, E.E. and Miller, E., [Eds.], *The Cambridge Economic History of Europe,* volume II, Cambridge, 1952; volume III, Cambridge, 1961, reprint Cambridge, 1971.

Prawdin, Michael, *The Mongol Empire : Its Rise and Legacy,* English Translation by Eden and Ceden Paul, London, 1961.

Qundus, Syed Abdul, *Punjab: The Land of Beauty, Love and Mystitcism,* Karachi, 1992.

Rachewelty, Igor de, ed., *The Secret History of the Mongols: A Mongolian Epic Chonical with Thirteenth Century,* 2 vols. Leiden and Boston: Brill, 2004.

Rahman, Afzal-ur, *Economic Doctrines of Islam,* London, 1980.

Rahul, Ram, *March of Central Asia,* New Delhi, 2002.

Rashid A., *Society and Culture in Medieval India,* Calcutta, 1969.

Ratchuevsky, Paul, *Genghis Khan: His Life and Legacy,* Translated by Thomas Nivison Haibning, Cambridge, 1992.

Raverty, H.G. Major, *Notes on Afghanistan and parts of Baluchistan,* London, 1880.

Ray, Himanshu Prabha, *Monastery and Guild,* O.U.P., 1986.

Reischaur, Edwin O. and Fairbank, John K., *East Asia: The Great Tradition,* Boston, 1960.

Richards, D.S. [Ed.], *Islam and the Trade of Asia,* Philadelphia, 1970.

Rizvi, S.A.A., *Aadi Turk Kalin Bharat,* Aligarh, 1956.

—, *Khalji Kalin Bharat,* Aligarh, 1955.

—, *Tughluq Kalin Bharat,* Aligarh, Part I, 1956 and Part II, 1957.

—, *Uttar Timur Kalin Bharat,* Aligarh, Part I, 1958 and Part II, 1959

Robinson, Francis, [Ed.] *The Cambridge Illustrated History of the Islamic World,* Cambridge, 1996.

Rossabi, Morris, [Ed.] *China Among Equals,* Berkeley, 1983.

Khubilai Khan: His Life and Times, California, 1988.

Said, Hakim Mohammed and Ansar Zahid Khan, *Al-Biruni: His Times, Life and Works,* Karachi, 1981.

Saunders, J.J., *The History of the Mongol Conquests,* London, 1971..

Schofield, Victoria, *Afghan Frontier: Feuding and Fighting in Central Asia,* New York, 2003.

Sharma, R.S. *Indian Feudalism,* Reprint, New Delhi, 1985.

Siddiqui, I.H., *Some Aspects of Afghan Despotism in India,* Aligarh, 1969.

Perso-Arabic Sources of Information on the Life and Conditions in the Sultanate of Delhi, New Delhi, 1992.

Silverstein, Adam J., *Postal Systems in the Pre-Modern Islamic World,* Cambridge, 2007.

Simikin, C.G.F., *The Traditional Trade of Asia,* Oxford, 1968.

Singh, Attar, [Ed.] *Socio-Cultural Impact of Islam in India,* Chandigarh, 1976.

Sinor, Denis [Ed.], *The Cambridge History of Early Inner Asia,* Cambridge, 1990.

Skrine, Francis Henry and Edward Denison Ross, *The Heart of Asia,* London, a reprint of 1899,London, 2004.

Spate, O.H.K., *India and Pakistan,* reprint, London, 1964.

Spain, James, *Pathan Borderland,* Hague, 1963.

Spector, Ivar, *An Introduction to Russian History and Culture,* Reprint, New York, 1950.

Spular, Bertold, *The Muslim World: Historical Survey* Part I: The Age of the Caliphs, Part II: *The Mongol Period,* Translation from German by F.R.C. Bagley, Leiden, 1960.

History of the Mongols based on the Eastern and Western accounts of the thirteenth and fourteenth centuries, Berkeley, 1972.

The Mongols in History, Translalated by Geoffrey Wheeler, London, 1971.

Steadman, M., John, *The Myth of Asia,* New York, 1969.

Steensgaard, Niels, *The Asian Trade Revolution of the Seventeenth Century,* London, 1974.

Steingass, F., *Persian English Dictationary,* Delhi,

Strange, G.Le, *The Lands of the Eastern Caliphate,*Cambridge, 1930.

—, *Baghdad during the Abbasid Caliphate,Oxford,* 1924.

Swinson, Arthur, *North West Frontier,* London, 1967.

Sykes, Percy, *A History of Persia,* I, London, 1969.

Tanner, Stephan, *Afghanistan: A Military History from Alexander the great to the fall of the Taliban,* New York, 2002.

Tchitcherov, Alexander, I., *India: Changing Economic Structure in the Sixteenth to Eighteenth Centuries,* Delhi, 1998.

Temple, Richard, *Oriental Experience,* Reprint, Delhi, 1986.

Thaksten, *The Mongol Conquests* AD 1200-1300, Times Life Books, Amsterdam.

Tracy, James D., *The Rise of Merchant Empires : Long-Distance Trade in the Early Modern World 1350-1750,* [Ed.], Cambridge, 1990.

Tucker, Jonathan, *The Silk Road: Art and History,* Timeless Books, New Delhi, 2003.

Vambery Arminis, *History of Bukhara,* London, 1873.

Verma H.C., *Medieval Routes to India,* Calcutta, 1978.

- *Dynamics of Urban Life in Pre-Mughal India,* Delhi, 1986.

Vernadsky, George, *The Mongols and Russia,* Yale, 1953.

Vladimirtsov, B.Ya, *The Life of Chingis Khan,* English translation from the Russian by Prince D.S., Nmirsky, London, 1930.

Warikoo, K., *Central Asia: Emerging New Order* [Ed.], New Delhi, 1995.

Weatherford, Jack, *Genghis Khan and the Making of the Modern World,* New York, 2004.

Williams, L.F. Rushbrook, *The State of Pakistan,* London, 1966.

Wink, Andre, *Al-Hind: The Making of the Indo-Islamic World:*

—, Vol. I *Early Medieval India and the Expansion of Islam, 7th-11th Centuries,* Oxford, 1990.

—, Vol. II *The Slave Kings and the Islamic Conquest, 11th-13th Centuries,* Leiden, 1997.

Wright, H.N. *The Coinage and Metrology of the Sultans of Delhi,* New Delhi, 1974.

Yadav, B.N.S., *Society and Culture in Northern India in the Twelfth Century,* Allahabad, 1973.

Yule, Henry (Translated and Edited), *Road to Cathay and Thirther* being a collection of Medieval Notices of China in 4 volumes, London, 1913-16.

Zamcarano, C.Z., *The Mongol Chroniclers of the Seventeenth Century,* English Translation by Rudolf Loewenthol, Wiesbaden, 1955.

JOURNALS, PROCEEDINGS, GAZETTERS AND ENCYCLOPAEDIAS ETC.

Acta Asiatica

Asia

Asia Major

Asian Affairs Asian Review

Bulletin of the School of Oriental Studies [London]

Central Asian Review

Central Asian Survey

E.J. Brill's First Encyclopedia of Islam

Economic and Political Weekly

Encyclopedia Britannica

Encyclopedia of Islam
Gazetteers of North-West Frontier Province
Harward Journal of Asiatic Studies
Hobson-Jobson
Imperial Gazetteers of Afghanistan and Nepal [1908]
Imperial Gazetteer of India
Indian Antiquary
Indian Historical Quarterly
Indian Historical Review
Indo-Iranica
International Economic History Congress
Iran
Islam and Modern Age
Islamic Culture
Journal of Asia and African Studies—Journal of Asian History
Journal of Asian Studies
Journal of Asiatic Society of Bengal
Journal of Central Asian Studies
Journal of Economic and Social History of the Orient
Journal of Oriental Studies
Journal of Royal Asiatic Society
Journal of the Bihar Research Society
Past and Present
Patna University journal [1963]
Proceedings of the Indian History Congress
Proceedings of the Punjab History Conference

Index